KOREAN KARATE

Free Fighting Techniques

Sihak Henry Cho

KOREAN KARATE

Free Fighting Techniques

CHARLES E. TUTTLE COMPANY: PUBLISHERS
RUTLAND, VERMONT   TOKYO, JAPAN

Representatives
Continental Europe: BOXERBOOKS, INC., *Zurich*
British Isles: PRENTICE-HALL INTERNATIONAL, INC., *London*
Australasia: PAUL FLESCH & CO., PTY. LTD., *Melbourne*
Canada: HURTIG PUBLISHERS, *Edmonton*

Published by the Charles E. Tuttle Company, Inc.
of Rutland, Vermont & Tokyo, Japan
with editorial offices at
Suido 1-chome, 2-6, Bunkyo-ku, Tokyo, Japan

Copyright in Japan, 1968 by Charles E. Tuttle Co., Inc.

Library of Congress Catalog Card No. 68-18608

International Standard Book No. 0-8048-0350-1

First edition, 1968
Tenth printing, 1974

Book design by Keiko Chiba
PRINTED IN JAPAN

Table of Contents

Foreword

THE TERM "karate" is a generalized term of Japanese origin, coined to represent the various traditional and modern styles of the so-called "empty-hand" combat art.

In Korea, *tae-kwon do* has only recently been agreed upon as the term representing modern Korean karate, superceding such terms as *tang-soo do*, *kong-soo do*, *tae-soo do*, *soo-bak do*, etc. Since *tae-kwon do* refers only to modern karate, it would be inaccurate to use it as a generic term throughout the entire manuscript.

Consultations with fellow *tae-kwon do* masters have convinced me that the term "karate" has become more widely known in Western countries than any other and would thus be a more familiar one to English-speaking peoples than would *tae-kwon do*. For this reason, I have decided to use "karate" throughout the entire book and "tae-kwon do" only where necessary to indicate the differentiation.

I wish to express my sincere appreciation to my students Robert Zychski, Carlos Farrell, and Julio LaSalle for posing with me in the photos to help make this book more expressive; to Charles Peck, Nat Greenspan, and Jerome Cohen for their unlimited advice and help in proofreading the entire manuscript; and to Bernard MacSweeney for his excellent photographs.

New York City   Sihak Henry Cho

9

Introduction

UNTIL approximately ten years ago, karate (*tae-kwon do*)* was practiced only in Far Eastern countries. Since then, it has gained such widespread attention that the whole world is becoming familiar with it. Its popularity in the United States has been brought about by many public demonstrations—by experts on TV, in public appearances, and in championship tournaments—as well as through books. However, there are still thousands interested in this art who do not know the real principles of karate. In fact, a number of unqualified karate demonstrators have given such an erroneous impression of it that many people believe that it is either a brutal method of killing people or an esoteric form of magic that gives the initiate an enormous power to destroy anything within reach of his hand.

Karate is a fighting art which employs almost all parts of the body in offensive and defensive moves. Karate techniques consist of many individual moves which are practiced as individual units and joined together for maximum efficiency in free fighting. These practice units are: basic drill in stances, kicking, punching, striking, blocking, combinations of these moves in formal patterns, prearranged attacks and counterattacks, stepping and shifting, etc. The combination of all of these results in skill at karate techniques, which is demonstrated in free fighting. Some of the moves are directly applicable to free fighting while the others develop basic speed and coordination.

One's ability to use these basic moves after they have been perfected can be seen in free fighting. Skill at free fighting is the main goal of karate, and its techniques are the karate techniques. The trainee cannot be good at karate just by learning the moves. He must train and drill extensively until each technique becomes reflexive, and he develops speed, power, accuracy, and balance. Such continued, conscientious training not only results in the ultimate in self-defense but also in a mental discipline which creates the strength of character necessary for success in all fields of endeavor.

This book is intended to fill the void in martial arts writing which has been discovered by all serious karate students and instructors as well as others interested in the sport. There have been a dozen karate books published in the English language, but none of them explain clearly the *how, why, when,* and *where* of the application of each karate move to free fighting. In this book, each move has been explained to the smallest detail so that even those working without instruction can profit by following it in their training. Also, the advantages and disadvantages of each technique are explained and many examples are cited which will give the reader a clear picture of practical values.

This book has been tailored for the competition karate practi-

* See Foreword

tioners because of the increased interest in championship matches throughout the world. It is hoped that it will serve as a basic instruction manual of free-fighting techniques for students and instructors, as a detailed guide for those interested in karate who are unable to have qualified instruction, and to enable the casual spectator to enjoy competition sparring through an awareness of exactly what is taking place.

Finally, this book answers the question asked by many people: "What is the difference between Korean and Japanese karate?" We find some differences in the training methods of the various schools and associations in each geographical area, but the basic difference is in the unique philosophy followed by each nation. However, while the schools remain apart in thought and styles, they are bound together by the practice of sparring, which is the only standard value in the sport recognized by all who are responsible for advancing the true art of karate.

Part I The Development of Karate

1 Historical Background

THE ORIGIN of karate as a simple form of self-defense is somewhat obscure, because ever since the beginning of mankind there have no doubt always been some forms of fighting techniques. Many, however, agree that karate as a martial art had its earliest beginnings in India thousands of years ago, where it reached a high stage of development. Indian folklore, history, dance, and drama make much of individual warriors, princes, and gods who accomplished mighty battlefield feats with their bare hands. Karate forms can also be seen in many works of art and particularly in temple sculptures which show warriors in positions similar to those of karate today.

Karate as a true martial art form was brought to China about 1500 years ago by the Indian Buddhist monk, Bodhidharma (Daruma), and it was studied with the emphasis on mental and physical development. Bodhidharma taught karate to the Chinese monks at the monastery of Shaolin-ssu whose residents later became famous as the foremost champions of fighting techniques throughout China. Undoubtedly, karate must have been accepted as a formal activity among the religious people and, furthermore, was widely developed among many other people at the time. It was the first time in its history that karate received notice, and its distinctive purpose was for self-defense and as an aid in enlightening the mind.

As time passed and karate became known as a lethal weapon, karate techniques began to be applied for offensive purposes in national wars or in internal conflicts caused by political upheaval. Many karate students traveled throughout northern and southern China, and trained military groups of many organized societies in the martial arts. A formal karate-training school for the furtherance of military training in this original art was thus established. These societies were the prime force in the Boxer Rebellion, and most of them are still in existence. In this tradition, karate masters commanded unarmed villages capable of applying karate techniques for offensive purposes in local conflicts and to meet the national crisis of war.

Once karate techniques were applied to war, as is to be expected, they were quickly adopted by many neighboring countries for both offensive and defensive purposes. Many countries, which had had their own fighting forms, accepted the scientifically developed karate movements, giving their own natural toughness to it, changing the techniques in the way best suited to their own national character. For a long period of time from then on, karate was developed in many places by many different authorities under many different philosophies and ideologies.

Characteristically, karate techniques were mainly applied for defensive purposes, as can be seen throughout its history. Karate, with its scientific body movements, came to be known as a lethal weapon which could be used against abusive laws; therefore, it was not welcomed by the rulers of the country and was developed secretly in many different geographical regions, from which came the different karate styles seen today. At this time, the major purpose of karate training was defense against injustice; the trainees' imaginary opponents were the thieves and bandits who used weapons against the common people who were forbidden by law to possess them.

"Okinawa-te" is one of those karate styles which developed historically and emerged as a distinct style. Karate was introduced to Okinawa by 17th-century Chinese warriors and missionaries and was superimposed on the original Okinawan-fighting system. The prime concern of the people was that karate techniques enabled them to protect themselves without the prohibited weapons, when the law itself was not strong enough or not sufficiently enforced to protect the rights of their families and themselves.

Through arduous study and by natural evolution, modern-day karate began to develop by the turn of the 20th century. It is basically rooted in its original techniques, but the enormous support of the people of many countries such as Japan, Okinawa, China, and Korea gave the impetus for the creation of a world-wide karate. Many different styles of karate are seen in modern times, but the philosophy of modern karate, embodying control, discipline, concentration of body and mind, sincerity and understanding is common to all styles. Under the leadership of many karate masters, such as Master Gichin Funakoshi who is directly responsible for the recent introduction of Okinawan karate into Japan, modern karate has been developed, giving rise to many professional karate practitioners all over the world.

2 *Tae-Kwon Do*, the Korean Karate

KOREAN karate (*tae-kwon do*) can be traced to *tae kyun*, a form of kicking- and leg-maneuvering exercise long a part of Korean history. Some authorities have stated that *tae kyun* was taught and practiced among Hwarang-do over 1000 years ago. Hwarang-do was organized as a national group of outstanding youths who were hand picked for training in swordsmanship and archery, and also to study to become military leaders of the country of Silla which was then one of the three ruling countries of Korea until all three were later unified by Silla in the 7th century.

It is assumed that *tae kyun* was practiced as part of the daily curriculum by the Hwarang-do, who lived deep in the mountains or near waterfalls enjoying the surroundings of nature, their daily life isolated from the confusion characteristic of the disorganized human society of that time. Initially, to those who were planning to be professional soldiers, ruling officials or leaders of the people, *tae kyun* was merely a form of bodily training and physical conditioning. As time passed, however, *tae kyun* is believed to have been influenced by karate which must have been introduced from the neighboring country of China. Before and after the powerful Tang (*Kara*) period of China, karate is assumed to have spread out into many countries throughout Asia along with the cultural exchange of Buddhism and other philosophies.

Tae kyun, which was not primarily based on the Buddhist doctrine, did not have national support during the period of the Koryu Kingdom of Korea (A.D. 918 to 1392). Koryu, which experienced a flowering Buddhist culture, became widely known throughout the world as Korea, which was derived from the pronunciation of Koryu. The reign of the Yi dynasty which followed the Koryu dynasty was unfortunately characterized by national chaos and social confusion which lasted for over 500 years until the beginning of the 20th century. The replacement of Buddhism by Confucianism at that time resulted in power struggles and ideological confusion. During this period, it is believed that *tae kyun* was practiced by a small select group who did not share their *expertise* with the people at large. The modern karate of Korea, with very little influence from *tae kyun*, was born with the turn of the 20th century when it was imported directly from China and also from Okinawa through Japan.

3 *Tae-Kwon Do,* and Japanese Karate

"KARATE" is a Japanese pronunciation of two Chinese characters which literally mean "empty hand." Another set of two Chinese characters, meaning "Kara hand" (or "the hand of the Kara Kingdom"), which is the original word for karate, was widely used in Japan until two decades ago. The latter is the original Chinese word that represents the word "karate" in Far Eastern countries and is still used by some karate schools or associations in Korea and China. Many Koreans describe the martial art of karate as "Kara hand" rather than "empty hand." Chinese words are indicated by one or more characters and have almost the same meaning in Chinese, Korean, or Japanese, but are pronounced differently in the respective countries. The people of those lands can read both "Kara hand" and "empty hand" and understand both to be nearly the same, but no Chinese, for example, can understand them when they are pronounced "*tang soo*" or "*kong soo*" in Korea.

Kara of "Kara hand" is the name of one of the old provinces in China. The Kara Province later unified all China, and was known outside as the Kara Kingdom. During this period, there was frequent contact with Korea, Japan, and other neighboring countries with cultural exchanges and international wars. However, during the period of the Kara Kingdom, the principles of karate were widely introduced to the people and further studied and developed. The martial art form, which presumably originated in the Kara Kingdom, became a symbol of national prestige, regarded with awe both inside and outside old China. The name given to it was "the hand of the Kara Kingdom," implying the use of the empty hand as a weapon. Such a descriptive title of the art indicates understanding and acceptance of the philosophy of the art by the public in the Oriental world at that time.

Okinawa-te is another example of a word with a geographical association which was used in Japan for several hundred years. *Okinawa-te*, meaning "Okinawa hand," is apparently a form of karate that derived from the preceding karate of Kara Province and was slightly changed in concept for the needs of the Okinawan people of that time. Perhaps "Okinawa hand" describes the possession of the art by Okinawan people who lived in a territory under the control of Japan and who trained and practiced karate secretly for themselves.

It is only recently that "Kara hand" has changed to "empty hand" in Japanese terminology. In describing this new word, there is more of an emphasis on the art itself than on its historical roots. A scientific study of the art has brought a great change, not only in its technical aspects, but also in its philosophical background. The "empty hand" is still pronounced "karate" as it was when it was written with the characters meaning "Kara hand" and this may imply a newly devised form of karate which originated from "the hand of the Kara Kingdom."

Tae-kwon is the Korean word for karate recently adopted by the Korean Tae-Kwon do Federation. *Tae-kwon do* (*tae* meaning foot; *kwon*, fist; and *do*, martial art) is identical to Japanese karate, and the title is a literal description of an art consisting of foot and hand techniques. Some of the Korean public still use the "karate" pronunciation in conversation, but Korean karate schools or associations have adopted such names as *tang soo* ("Kara hand"), *kong soo* ("empty hand"), *tae soo* ("foot hand"), etc. Many Koreans acknowledge the art as *tang soo* which is the traditional Korean title and represents the origin of the art as the term "karate" does in Japan. Whatever the titles may be, they were chosen by individual schools as an attempt at a descriptive expression for the martial art as it relates to their own individual philosophies. However, in spite of the various philosophies in the long history of karate, it has now evolved into a completely modernized form; its basic concept being the building of karate practitioners with the strongest techniques of sportsmanlike self-defense.

The karate title of "empty hand" and the *tae-kwon do* of "foot-hand" may give different impressions of the same art. The "empty hand" of unarmed fighting suggests more of an emphasis on self-defense techniques, whereas the "foot-hand" of foot and hand fighting implies a physical training of various techniques using the whole body. The latter more closely represents the sport of karate but it lacks the historical implications. Many Westerners, misunderstanding the term "empty hand" fighting, assume the feet play no part in karate techniques.

4 *Tae-Kwon Do,* the Modern Karate

MODERN karate or *tae-kwon do* consists of the techniques of body movement executed with maximum power, speed, accuracy, and balance. Training in karate provides the trainee with an ability to impart a momentary focus of power, derived from muscle contraction of the body along with mental concentration. The power of a strike, punch, kick, or block is increased through constant practice to the point where the trainee converts his entire potentiality into actual ability. The entire potential force is focused and increased in its application with the help of appropriate body twisting, reaction force where one hand retreats as the other extends, speed of the delivery, and other techniques. Speed, which plays an important part in karate techniques, must be constantly built on the basis of simple unit moves which are applied in a combined form with body shifting. Speed without power is completely ineffective. The degree of both power and speed is always affected by the target of the movement because the effect of a punch directed to the opponent's eyes, for example, is more damaging than the same punch directed against the chin. The sense of balance is always important as in any other physical activity because it brings coordination. Strict training in the execution of definitive movements both in offense and defense is what makes karate superior to simpler means of fighting, and coordination and conditioned responses are among the most important elements of karate techniques.

Modern karate is a physical science. In karate training, individual unit movements of the entire body are perfected to be joined together as one for effective application through a systematic procedure. The trainee first practices each unfamiliar body movement by himself against an imaginary target until the movement becomes a meaningful part of his techniques applicable to an actual opponent. Karate techniques, which can be constantly improved, are always evaluated on the basis of the scientific applications of its principles embodying reflexes and coordination.

Modern karate is a sport. In general, the uniformity of performance of techniques and their evaluation on the basis of karate concepts set a standard of achievement for all karate trainees. Therefore, the techniques are always competitive. Ever since the wide acceptance of modern karate, there have been many karate free-fighting matches under rules and regulations of control. The point system of the karate free-fighting matches was devised specifically with limitations of striking areas in order to measure the skill and ability of body movements.

Modern karate, is a physical fitness. The training necessary to perfect each movement requires the muscular exercise of the whole body and ultimately provides the best means for physical fitness. Each movement builds muscular coordination, and sincere and constant training can develop the muscles of the whole body.

Modern karate is a martial art. In its application as a means of self-defense, its techniques have killing effectiveness. Each body movement is designed for combat needs, and the concentrated mental and physical force can cause extreme damage to the opponent. Mental discipline, self-confidence, and self-control bring to karate trainees the utmost determination and stability of both mind and body.

Modern karate is the discipline of both mind and body. Its body movements are new to beginners but they must practice these constantly until they become natural to them. Each movement should not be applied until it is nearly perfected. Because karate is a martial art, karate trainees must first distinguish right from wrong. Self-control is achieved through the philosophy of "respect the Elder and love the Younger" and this leads into self-understanding. Karate techniques and their application look easy but are hard to learn. Discipline is necessary for the trainee so that he will study to improve his techniques and develop his potentiality to the point where they can be utilized in application, and as his physical ability increases so does his mental control and focus.

Modern karate is world-wide karate. The principles of karate can be and have been accepted by many different races of the world because the concept of karate is adaptable to many different ideologies. Karate is so universal in scope that it belongs to all races and creeds. Karate techniques, stressing mental and physical discipline, can be adjusted to some degree for different ages, sizes, and professions. Karate, as its history shows, is expected to change and grow without remaining in a pure form. As each nation develops and adds to a particular phase of karate to make it most suitable to its community, as each school develops certain special techniques of its own, and as each master prefers certain movements, the techniques of karate will

continue to change but its essential principles and traditional philosophy will form the framework upon which the modifications will rest.

Part II Calisthenics and Stances

5 Calisthenics

CALISTHENICS are related to karate moves, as they are body-conditioning exercises, and body conditioning is one of the most important functions of karate training. The karate function of body conditioning is achieved through intensive training of various moves, which require the maneuvering of most parts of the body. Calisthenics themselves can also be body conditioning if they are performed in such a manner that the exercise is greater than a simple warming-up. As in any other sport, karate trainees are advised to do calisthenics in order to loosen up muscles and joints before and after performing the strenuous karate moves. In addition to exercises to loosen up such joints as the wrist, elbow, and ankle, along with many other ways of general calisthenics, some typical karate calisthenics will be briefly explained.

● Neck Exercise

Slowly move your head back and forth, turn it side to side or all the way around in a circular motion, or press it down sideway toward the shoulder. These exercises will relax one from tension and serve as both neck and head exercises.

● Shoulder Exercise

Raise your arms all the way up pressing backward while stretching the front part of your body. Then continue the exercise by dropping your arms downward, pressing them backward, or you may first place both arms in an X-position in front of your body and then raise them in a circular motion in order to exercise your chest and shoulder muscles.

● Back and Forth Exercise

Do not bend your knees while moving your upper body back and forth. This provides back and stomach exercise and usually relaxes you. Avoid pressing too much.

● Side Exercise

This exercise is for the side of your body. Do not bend your knees or hip joint. Bend only the side part of your upper body.

● Twisting Exercise

This exercise is to avoid muscle strain while twisting your body in training. Keep your feet firmly on the floor, twisting your body slowly from your knees to the shoulders. Twist your upper body from left to right and right to left, placing your arms at a low, middle, and high level. You may circle around, relaxing the midsection of your body and knee area while twisting. The twisting exercise for the knees will avoid any possible strain on your supporting knee while kicking.

Once you loosen up the entire upper body, you may try a sudden and forceful twisting.

● Hip Exercise

Exercise hip joint by moving the hip back and forth, then side to side, and then all the way around in a circular motion.

● Knee Exercise

Slowly squat down and stand up, maintaining both feet flat on the floor and upper body upright. The wider the distance between your two feet, the harder it is to squat down. This provides exercise for the thigh muscles and hip joints.

● Leg-Stretching Exercise

For front kick, stretch out one leg at a time, pointing the toes up and for side kick, pointing the outer edge of the foot up. While stretching, keep the supporting foot flat on the floor. You may stretch both legs at the same time by doing the "split" when you become good enough.

● Push-Up Exercise

In general, push-ups are very good exercise for conditioning the body. You may do it with one hand or two, on the palm-heels or first two knuckles, or even on the finger tips. You may do your push-ups fast or slowly. Make sure the entire body moves in a straight line when you press up and down.

● Loosening-Up Exercise

If preferred, two trainees can get together and help each other in loosening up the upper body. This type of exercise is good before and after training. Avoid any sudden pulling which might cause a strain.

6 Stances *(Chwa Seh)*

● Natural Stance (*Cha-yun Seh*)

Any stance which feels natural to the average person is a natural stance. It is a relaxed posture with the upper body straight and shoulders natural.

The position in the front line (picture above) is the standard natural stance. Both legs are usually straight within the body line, feet about shoulder width apart, and arms extended slightly forward.

● Horseback-Riding Stance (*Kee-mah Seh*)

This stance is used for a finishing blow in full power as it provides a very strong base for attacks as well as blocks. Since this is a static stance, one cannot easily move away from or into his opponent using it. This stance is, however, important as a training stance that provides strong balance.

Step sideward with your left foot about twice the standard natural stance width, both feet exactly on a line and hold them stationary. Bend your knees outward and sink down as if mounted on a horse. The hips should be pushed to the rear with your upper body straight, and centered in the middle of both legs. Head and eyes face straight ahead. The chest is open and shoulders relaxed while all muscles on the legs through the hips remain tense. Both feet stay flat on the floor parallel to each other.

● Side Stance (*Yup Seh*)

The side stance is the same as the horseback-riding stance only it is executed when the opponent is on the side. Very often a short side stance (which is the same as the horseback-riding stance but with the distance between both feet about one and a half times that in the standard natural stance), is used for fast pick-up purposes while stepping or turning on the side. The use of the side stance in free fighting leaves a limited opening for the opponent's counterattack. It is natural to use the side stance as a base when executing side kicks and side punches.

Straight Stepping in Side Stance. Assuming the opponent is on your left side, move into him by bringing your right foot over your left, stepping behind the left, or on a straight line to the side, and pushing out to the left. Reverse the procedure for moving away.

Pivot Stepping in Side Stance. This stepping is executed by pushing off with front or rear foot and pivoting either forward or backward in a tight circle toward or away from the opponent. Keep watching the opponent while turning in either direction. Your knees and hips should always be kept bent as they are in the static position and your head remains on the same level while stepping.

● Forward Stance (*Chun-gool Seh*)

Forward stance is used for both stationary techniques and for moving in a back or forth direction. This stance provides a means of stepping a comparatively long distance in which the advancing motion of the body provides an additional forward force for punches, strikes, kicks, and blocks. Many find moving in this stance unnatural in the beginning but constant training makes the stance smooth and natural. Forward stance in actual application leaves wide openings on the body, but it provides the strongest body movements and balance. This is one of the most frequently used stances in basic drill.

To make the forward stance from the natural stance, move your right foot diagonally back to a distance of about twice the width of your shoulders. The width of the lines between your left and right feet is about the same as with the original ready position in natural stance. Both feet stay flat on the floor. Your front toes face straight forward and the knee is bent with the lower part of the leg straight up. The toes of your rear foot point in an approximate 30-degree angle to your right, the knee is straight, and the right hip is pushed forward. Your upper body is straight in a front-facing posture with the arms relaxed but the chest is widely open. The distribution of the body weight is about 60 per cent on the front foot and 40 per cent on the rear foot. A half-front facing posture is sometimes made in forward stance.

Stepping in Forward Stance. To step forward from forward stance, first bring your rear foot to the front so your body advancement is made with a natural motion. Then, continue to extend the rear foot forward at about a 30-degree angle toward your right, with the knee slightly bent. While stepping, the right foot travels forward only slightly off the floor with the left knee remaining bent until it locks to straighten the whole leg at the last minute. At the same time the front foot is placed on the floor. The distance and width of the feet in the new forward stance must be about the same as in the previous one.

When a middle punch accompanies the stepping in forward stance, the position of both arms with relation to the body posture remains unchanged, and only when the right foot returns to the floor is the punch delivered with the other hand cocking back. When stepping backward, the whole move begins by bending the rear knee first and repeating the same procedure in reverse direction.

● Back Stance (*Hoo-gool Seh*)

The distance between the front and rear feet in back stance is shorter than in forward stance and longer than in cat stance, which will be explained in the following section. Therefore, it is applied as an intermediate-distance stance in free fighting. Both offensive and defensive body movements are executed from the back stance, and it is usually made with the body in either a half-front or side-facing posture, although a front-facing posture is occasionally used. This stance generally provides more flexible body movement than forward stance because of the shorter distance between the two legs. Back stance is primarily a mobile stance and is often used in basic form practice. Many karate styles prefer back stance as the main free-fighting stance, because it is easy to shift from it to either a long-distance or short-distance stance.

How to Make Back Stance. To make back stance from a natural-stance ready position, bring your right foot back to form a right angle with the front foot. The distance between the front and rear feet is about one and a half shoulder widths, and the heels of both front and rear feet lie on a straight line toward the opponent, with the front toes facing forward and the rear toes to the right. Both feet stay flat on the floor. The rear leg, hips, and body are on an almost vertical line. The front knee is bent, but it is pressed toward the body to push the body weight toward the rear leg. Therefore, the front foot extends from the body farther than the knee. The upper body stays straight upright whether in a front, half-front, or side-facing posture. About 70 per cent of the body weight is supported by the rear leg.

Stepping in Back Stance. Details of stepping in back stance are covered in later chapters dealing with its application to free fighting. However, some points are worth remembering in order to practice basic-stepping movements.

Any punches, strikes, blocks, and kicks can be effectively practiced while moving in back stance. Stepping from one back stance to another is relatively easier than moving in forward stance, because the distance of stepping is not so great as to require an extra body maneuver. Therefore, the weight transfer is made smoothly in back stance, as both knees are already bent, which makes the stepping smoother by moving the whole body on a straight line without the necessity for raising or lowering it. Caution must be taken to maintain most of the body weight on the rear leg while punching or kicking following the stepping. Avoid the unconscious transfer of the weight to the front foot while striking or punching forward, through lack of control of the thrusting force.

● Cat Stance (*Tuit-bal Seh*)

Cat stance is made with a narrow distance between the front and rear feet. The body is usually in a front- or half-front facing posture, although a side posture can be used. This stance is most often used for defensive or counterattacking purposes. Some karate styles prefer cat stance to other stances and use it often, because it generally gives a fast pick-up for body shifting and for delivering a kick with the front foot without telegraphing it, since there is almost no weight resting on this foot. However, the body movements executed in cat stance are generally weak because of the short distance through which the move travels, the uneven weight distribution and the lack of body advancement in stepping. Needless to say, cat stance is also a mobile stance.

How to Make Cat Stance. To make cat stance from a natural-stance ready position, bring the right foot directly behind the left foot, so the feet almost touch. Most of the body weight rests on the rear foot which is flat on the floor with the knee slightly bent, while the ball of the front foot simply touches the floor so that it can be easily lifted without shifting the body weight. Tense the rear knee inward to support the forward body direction.

● Others

In addition to those karate stances we have covered, there are many others which are often used in training: even stance, inward bent knee stance, low stance, and short forward stance will be briefly explained in this section.

Even Stance (*Koroo Seh*). A good example of even stance is side stance; the body weight rests evenly on both front and rear feet. However, even stance is often used in free fighting as a variation of back stance. The toes of both feet point inward, so that the whole body remains tense. The upper body stays straight upward in either a half-front facing or side-facing posture with the eyes watching straight forward along the left leg line. This type of stance can be used in free fighting as a static stance to arm block or guard in a tight position against your opponent's offense, without making a defensive body shift.

Inward Bent Knee Stance (*Moorup Ohkoohryo Seh*). As a variation of even stance, inward bent knee stance is sometimes used in practicing karate (tae-kwon do) basics in a tense leg position. Both feet remain flat on the floor and toes point in an inward direction. Both knees are bent, tensing inward, with the front knee directly over the big toe of the front foot and the rear knee bending farther inward. The distance between the left and right feet can vary from that of natural stance to that of side stance, and both feet stay somewhere between the side and front direction. From this stance, short hand moves are primarily applied in a side or forward direction. Occasionally this type of stance is used in free fighting to make a sudden stop of the body advancement or to change the direction of motion for a continuous offense.

Low Stance (*Natchwoh Seh*). Low stance is an extension of forward stance primarily used for hand attacks with a thrusting motion. In general, the distance between the front and rear feet is longer, the diagonal distance between the left and right feet is shorter, and the upper body remains lower than in forward stance. This type of stance results from making a thrusting attack in free fighting, but it also can be used to cover a long distance and ultimately provides a stronger body advancement than regular forward stance. The weight distribution of the body between the long distance of both feet hinders a fast body shift, and the narrow distance between the feet makes the body balance weak from a side angle.

Short Forward Stance (*Pahn Chun-gool Seh*). As the name implies, short forward stance is very similar to forward stance except the distance between the front and rear feet is less, and the body is higher than in forward stance. The shorter distance between the feet usually provides better mobility for shifting. Because of the shorter distance, the rear knee can sometimes be bent slightly.

Part

III

Part III Free Fighting Basics and Foot Moves

7 Basic Position and Adjustment for Distance

The karate (*tae-kwon do*) trainee should not free fight until he masters the basic karate moves to the point where they can be used instinctively in any free-fighting situation. In order to master these basic moves, he usually practices them alone, assuming an imaginary opponent before him. However, such practice is quite different from the application of these moves against an actual opponent in free fighting. The real opponent presents a moving target, in contrast to an imaginary opponent or stationary bag. The real opponent can also attack the trainee, who must be prepared to make both offensive and defensive moves. In other words, the actual free fighting techniques of the trainee are his ability not only to execute simple karate moves, but also to effectively apply both offensive and defensive moves in free fighting.

The karate free-fighting position is somewhat different from the fighting positions of boxing, wrestling, or judo, because the karate attack is not limited to the fist alone as in boxing, or a throw as in wrestling or judo, but utilizes the finger tips, palm-heel, knife-edge, elbow, and many varied foot techniques. In addition, many defensive techniques are also applied in order to protect the numerous vulnerable spots of the body. Most of all, the combination of strong hand-and-foot attacks requires a strong body balance, and the effective application of defensive moves, along with offensive moves, requires good coordination and superb balance to be advantageously applied in free fighting.

The main free-fighting stance must be one which provides an intermediate distance between both feet to facilitate complete mobility. Back stance, even stance, short side stance, or short forward stance are better to start with than forward stance or low stance, which provide a strong balance but lack mobility because the body balance is spread between the front and rear feet. Cat stance usually allows a fast pick-up of the front foot for kicking, but the short distance between the feet might result in a weak foundation for both hand and foot techniques. However, the main free-fighting stance must be changed from time to time from cat stance to back stance, short forward stance, even stance, and so forth, depending upon the moves you want to make.

A half-front facing posture is preferable to a front- or side-facing posture in free fighting. The front-facing posture is usually good for attacking with the hands and feet, but it exposes the front part of the body and is a disadvantageous posture for defense. A side-facing posture leaves less of an opening and is safer for defense, but limits offensive moves and lacks advancing force. The half-front facing posture is best suited as an intermediate position for both offense and defense.

The body should always be erect and relaxed and the eyes should look directly at the opponent. Do not watch his legs or hands for indications of his movements, but rather his eyes. The front-guarding arm is held at the front-body line with the elbow bent and shoulder relaxed. The fist is tight and stays no higher than the shoulder level. The forearm is slightly inside the body line so it guards the front-facing ribs. The rear arm is held in front of the body with the fist somewhere around the solar plexus. The guarding position of both arms is approximately at the midsection of the body, from which they can be raised or lowered to protect other sections of the body. The knife-hand edge may be used instead of the fist. You must always be in a tightly guarded position whether you remain stationary or move. Be sure not to allow your opponent to induce you to relax your guard. While attacking, always move in a guarded position to protect yourself against the opponent's potential counter moves.

● Vital Spots of the Human Body

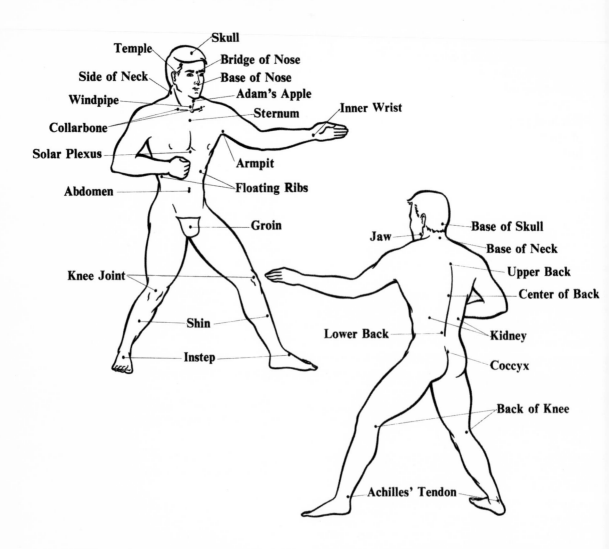

Skull
Temple
Bridge of Nose
Side of Neck
Base of Nose
Windpipe
Adam's Apple
Sternum
Inner Wrist
Collarbone
Solar Plexus
Armpit
Abdomen
Floating Ribs
Groin
Knee Joint
Shin
Instep

Jaw
Base of Skull
Base of Neck
Upper Back
Center of Back
Lower Back
Kidney
Coccyx
Back of Knee
Achilles' Tendon

● Adjustment for Distance

Many otherwise well-executed attacking moves are wasted because of the improper distance between the attacker and his opponent. Consequently, the attacker expends his energy senselessly. In general, karate practitioners maintain the free-fighting distance between each other that is either favorable to their own moves, or such that the opponent is in an unfavorable position to make an initial attack. The distance maintained must be slightly beyond reach of a simple attack with hands or feet. An initial attack from such a defensive distance should be preceded by closing the distance so that the attack can reach the specified target.

The adjustment for distance is an offensive step performed by extending the front foot or by bringing the rear foot forward or sideway. It primarily precedes a simple stepping or attacking move. The adjustment for distance gives the proper distance and direction for the execution of a successful attack. While adjusting, the attacker estimates the fighting distance and assumes the correct body posture, depending upon the type of attack to follow. A successful attack can be made from an oblique direction following a proper adjustment for distance when an opening from that direction is detected. Adjustment for distance enables an advancing force to be added to the attacking move. The adjustment for distance will be applied in detail in many different moves in later sections.

Extending the Front Foot. This adjustment for distance is performed by extending the front foot in a forward or oblique direction, shortening the distance between you and your opponent in order to follow through with rear hand or foot attacks. A simple attacking move follows the extension of the front foot forward. This type of adjustment is used in a same-side facing position where one leads with his left leg and the other with his right in order to attack the solar plexus, for example, and in an opposite-side facing position both leading with same leg to attack the front-facing kidney.

Push your front foot forward as far as necessary to adjust for the right distance between you and your opponent and attack with the reverse hand or foot. This is a simple method of shortening the distance and provides a strong advancing force for the attack. While adjusting, your free-fighting position is primarily unchanged. Therefore, a rapidly executed adjusting move may not be detected by the opponent.

Bringing the Rear Foot Forward. This is an adjustment for distance made by first bringing the rear foot forward and then attacking with the front hand or foot. When the attack is made with the front hand, it is accompanied by the forward extension of the front foot. The rear foot must be brought to the spot from which an attack can be successfully executed.

To adjust for distance in order to attack with the front hand or foot, bring your rear foot forward and place it somewhere around or ahead of the front foot, depending upon how close to your opponent you must be for your attack to be successful. You can attain a side-facing posture for your attack by pointing the toes to the side as you bring up the rear foot.

A continuous adjustment can be made by repeating the same adjusting move after extending your front foot forward following the original adjustment for distance.

In free fighting, a combined adjustment for distance is often applied against the opponent who unexpectedly moves after detecting your original stepping move. Some examples of combination adjustments will be shown in later sections. It can be made easily by extending the front foot forward first and then bringing the rear foot forward again before initiating an attack.

● Fake

A fake is performed when a free fighter indicates that he is going to perform a certain move, solely for the purpose of drawing the opponent's attention to it, so he can then launch a real attack, catching the opponent off guard. For this reason a fake should be executed with a snappy but obvious motion with the hand, foot, or the entire body.

The reaction of the opponent to the fake may result in his changing his guarding position or commencing the execution of a block or shift, thereby rendering him less prepared to defend against a different actual attack. His defense against the fake may result in the creation of an opening for a rapid subsequent real attack.

If a particular fake is used several times the opponent may cease to react to it. It may then be possible to score with the very move which had been used as a fake previously. A fake move can indicate how the opponent customarily reacts, enabling you to plan your future strategy effectively.

The ability to employ the fake with *expertise* is an important part of many different successful karate combinations. Later sections will show specific applications of the fake.

8 Foot Moves

● Stepping (*Bal Ohmkigi*)

Karate trainees must acquire broad knowledge and training in free-fighting moves to enable them to understand their own moves as well as their opponents'. Free-fighting stepping is the method of body movement. The spirit of "Go get 'em" as it is taught in some schools may work once in a while but the mastery of stepping provides a bridge between knowledge and practical application. It can provide you with the ability to close in on your opponent and allows you to move into a position to create openings. Stepping should be practiced with the aim of making this free-fighting move, fast, strong, and natural.

Maintaining a correct and balanced free-fighting position is important whether you are stepping forward, backward, or sideway in both offense and defense. Unless you have mastered stepping, your offensive and defensive techniques can easily fail in application.

Simple Forward and Backward Stepping. This is one of the basic moves which must be practiced continuously for application in free fighting. You can practice stepping forward and backward in a single stance first. You can then vary this routine by practicing stepping from one stance into another. Drop your front-guarding arm slightly across your front-facing area until your rear foot passes the front foot. Then push your rear arm forward, simultaneously extending the rear foot forward. This step is made with a simple motion of body rotation. To step backward, you move in the same manner but reverse the procedure.

Straight Forward and Backward Stepping. When you step forward, first remove your body weight from your front foot and push your body forward with the rear foot. The front foot must be placed in the new stance as the rear foot pushes the body forward. When stepping backward, relieve your rear foot of weight by moving your center of gravity slightly forward and push your body backward with the front foot. The whole move must be executed as one simple stepping move whether it is to the front or rear.

Such a step does not have to cover a long distance. It is used to maintain the most advantageous distance for you, and you should always be ready to move either backward or forward. Continuous stepping can be used to adjust distance for both offense and defense.

Open Stepping. This movement is performed by extending the front foot outward in a 45- to 150-degree angle from the body line, with the position of the guarding arms switched while stepping in defense. If the new position after shifting is at a 90-degree angle from the original position, it is called "90-degree stepping"; 45-, 120-, or 150-degree stepping indicates the angle of the new position in relation to the original position. Since this type of stepping requires a big body maneuver, which opens your main target area, it should be executed rapidly. Whatever the direction or degree may be, the principles of stepping are the same, and your new position should be far enough away from the opponent so he cannot easily follow with another attack.

As illustrated above, guard your front-facing area with your front arm while stepping in a 135-degree angle. Also, move your rear foot in a line that faces the target directly or a safe place for your next move.

To make a 90-degree open step, lift your front foot and lean your upper body weight toward your new position. Then, push the entire body weight with the rear foot, drawing it up immediately. Both feet should land in the new position almost simultaneously, and a well-balanced and guarded free-fighting position should be assumed instantly. This way, you are prepared to block or move away from your opponent's combination attack.

Closed Stepping. The direction of this step is the opposite of open stepping. This step is made by moving the front foot inward across the body line and placing it at a 25- to 90-degree angle forward. The rear foot usually follows the front. This type of step is usually made when there is a short distance between you and your opponent. Characteristically, this movement is used for a fast counterattack after a short distance step away from the opponent's advance. Avoid the frequent application of this step in free fighting unless you become expert at it, since it can leave you in a vulnerable position with your back exposed to the opponent's continuous attack.

Bring your front foot across the body line, with your arms guarding your front-facing ribs and kidney. As soon as the foot lands on its new spot, follow with your rear foot so you face the opponent directly. While stepping with the front foot, you may make an arm block if necessary. This kind of step is particularly good against a thrusting attack from a side-facing position, and its use may put you into an advantageous position for fast counter moves.

Circle Stepping. This step is made by moving your rear foot outward in a circular direction while the front foot barely moves. Your arms must remain guarding the front-facing area of your body while stepping.

This type of step is primarily for defensive purposes. When you intend to make a fast counterattack or if you have no other choice against the opponent's unexpected attack, you can defend with circle stepping in order to hide the exposed area of your front body. However, this is an advanced movement that should only be applied in extreme circumstances, since it can result in a dangerous loss of balance. However, if it is performed with the front foot withdrawing slightly backward, this almost completely eliminates the possibility of destroyed balance, allowing you the proper position for a fast-following move.

Others. Some karate practitioners move around their opponents in a side direction by stepping to the side in order to create an opening. This type of step is sometimes advantageous because the opponent cannot easily detect one's intentions; therefore, he cannot easily score on the moving target. However, this can be a somewhat dangerous step if the direction is discovered, since one is in a very weak defensive position.

Another step which is frequently used among karate practitioners is spot stepping, which is better known as spot shifting. This is performed by lifting both feet simultaneously and moving either forward, backward, or sideway. This type of stepping is applied both offensively and defensively in free fighting, and is worthwhile to practice in the classroom. Sometimes, spot stepping leaves you in a weak position against a continued attack and also robs you of power. All types of multiple and combined stepping moves should be practiced until they become instinctive.

● Body Shifting (*Mohm Ohmkigi*)

Body shifting means an instant shifting of the total body weight while stepping forward, backward, sideway, or in a circular direction. Therefore, it is a combination of weight shifting and stepping. Many karate fighters attempt to use it, but frequently their lack of training results in an inability to perform this move correctly, placing them in an awkward position. To avoid such mistakes, it is essential that weight shifting always be accompanied by an appropriate step with the arms tightly guarding the front-facing area. Shifting increases both speed and force, giving maximum effectiveness to both offensive and defensive moves. Constant training in weight shifting, simple shifting, and other shifting, along with stepping is invaluable to all karate trainees.

Weight Shifting. Weight shifting is the shifting of body weight from one leg to the other or one side to the other. It is performed with a snapping motion of the whole body by moving or twisting the upper body, locking the rear knee and pushing with the hips. It is the most important part of body shifting, and it can be applied either alone or with stepping for powerful karate moves.

A good way to practice weight shifting is in combination with the reverse straight punch. Other hand moves can also be used. The right-hand reverse straight punch is delivered in even stance while the weight of the body is brought forward by twisting slightly to the left. At the same time, the additional twisting motion of the rear knee and hips adds forward momentum. You often end in forward stance as in the picture to the left because of the advancing force of the body.

Simple Shifting. Simple shifting is weight shifting accompanied by a simple step or extension of one of the legs forward, backward, or sideway. It is the body shift most often used to change from short-distance stances to long-distance stances. Constant training in many different variations will help to develop smooth, fast stepping and good body coordination.

In order to practice simple shifting in natural stance with a fist punch, cock the punching hand and twist the body slightly. Then, step forward by extending one foot, at the same time delivering the punch. Alternatively, you can make a front thrust kick while shifting forward. You must be in good balance when the shift and punch are completed.

You may repeat these moves over and over again with slight changes if desired. However, the body weight must be shifted as quickly as possible from one leg to the other. Instead of practicing shifting on both sides, practice on just one side, both forward and backward, until you master the move, and then practice on the other side.

Among the many variations of simple shifting practices, you can practice a punch or an arm block while first shifting the body weight from natural stance to side stance, and then shifting again into forward stance. Instead of returning to natural stance after the execution of the punch or block with the weight shifting, you can continue the practice by pushing the body weight all the way backward as fast as you can with the front foot and deliver a low block in forward stance (or push out forward with front thrust kick).

You can also practice simple body shifting in a free-fighting position. Assuming a cat-stance position, you can attack your opponent by extending the front leg toward him into forward stance, low stance, or other long-distance stances.

Spot Shifting. This is a common move of boxers, accomplished by hopping with both feet forward, backward, sideway, or in a circling direction for both offensive and defensive purposes. It is preferably performed from a natural-stance free-fighting position or other similar short-distance stance positions where the legs are close together, because the narrower the weight distribution is, the more quickly the body moves. This type of shifting gives a fast movement and is good against many hand attacks as well as kicks, but lacks strong balance. The speedy move of spot shifting is most helpful to shorten the distance between you and your opponent so you can attack unexpectedly. In defending, it serves to quickly increase the distance so the opponent's attack is rendered inaccurate. This type of shifting can often be applied to free fighting for a fast initial move and, as soon as the new position is reached, the fighter assumes a wide stance for stronger balance and power. Defensive spot shifting is generally weak against combined attacks, because the distance covered is short. Therefore, it is often combined with a second spot shift or another type of shift when applied in free fighting.

While spot shifting, care must be taken in timing and coordination. Both upper and lower portions of the body move together and a strong guard should be maintained with the knees slightly bent for good mobility. You must not jump too high in the air. To move quickly, your feet should be just off the ground. Do not attempt to cover too great a distance as your balance will be weak for a subsequent move.

Combined Shifting. A single-shifting move either in offense or defense is sometimes not adequate against the opponent's combination moves, and two or sometimes three shifting moves are needed to control the situation. Moreover, in free fighting, do not use the same shifting move all the time, for your opponent will be able to predict your moves and take advantage of them. However, combinations of three or more stepping moves can easily lead you into an unguarded or off-balanced position.

There are many ways shifting moves can be combined for effective application in free fighting. Two or more shifts of the same kind should be practiced. Examples of double straight shifting and 90-degree shifting moves are briefly explained.

When straight stepping is performed in more than one step, it is best to begin with a short step and make the final step as long as you need, because the smaller extension of your legs makes it easier to initiate a move in your chosen direction. By doing so, your body is always in a position to be quickly coordinated for the following step and to reach the opponent at the appropriate moment.

The characteristic of this type of stepping, be it single or combined, is that your upper body and arm guards do not have to be changed while stepping.

Another set of double shifts frequently used are two 90-degree shifts, which are used primarily for defensive purposes. This type of shift results in a zigzag move which is particularly good against a continuous straight line attack. Your defense becomes weak unless the shifting moves are performed at full speed with good coordination, at a safe distance from your opponent's attack. (In the picture below, the opponent's attacking move results in a combined form by his shifting straight forward first and then in a 45-degree forward angle.)

Two or more shifting moves of different kinds can be combined in many variations: simple forward and straight forward stepping, 100-degree open and straight backward stepping, circle and 90-degree open shifting, 90-degree open and simple backward stepping, straight forward and simple backward stepping, simple forward and closed shifting are examples from a virtually endless list of such combinations.

This constitutes an offensive move of simple forward shifting followed by closed shifting to move into a defensive position because the opponent has responded with an instant counterattack or unexpected moves. While shifting offensively, you must change your direction quickly as soon as you detect counter moves, or you must block his attacking moves. The change from offensive to defensive shifting in the above picture is made by changing your direction to a 45-degree angle on your left side.

Counter Shifting. Counter shifting is the combination of defensive body shifting followed by offensive body shifting. The defensive shift must have two results: safe defense from the opponent's initial attack and creation of an opening for a counterattack. The shift in a backward or sideway direction usually covers a long distance, resulting in a safe position. The offensive shift is usually performed with an adjustment for distance. Such unexpected counter shifting before the opponent recovers a defensive position following his unsuccessful attack frequently surprises him and catches him defenseless. The ability to shift in all directions at all times should be developed to the utmost, and mastery of it will leave you in a formidable defensive position.

Good speed, coordination, and reflexes are essential for successful counter moves. Counterattacks following the defensive moves of simple backward stepping, straight backward stepping, 90-degree open shifting, and other similar shifts are good examples of counter shifting, and these will be applied in later sections. Spot shifting can be effectively applied in many counter shifting situations.

An adjustment for distance prior to counter shifting should be applied whenever you find that the distance between you and your opponent is too great for your immediate counterattack. Your counterattacking move accompanied by a counter shifting, followed first by an adjustment for distance, might provide you an extra distance to compensate for, a result of his shifting away following his unsuccessful initial attack. An adjustment for distance with a faking motion prior to a counter shifting following your successful defense is also effective against an opponent who, while stepping away, often does an instant counterattack with his front hand or foot against your counter-shifting move.

Part IV Blocking Techniques
(Makgi)

BLOCKING in karate *(tae-kwon do)* generally means striking, deflecting, or pressing, the opponent's attacking hands or legs with the defender's blocking arms or feet. The "arm block" is a block delivered with the arm and the "foot block," with the leg or foot. The arm block can be divided into the basic arm block and the applied arm block. Some of the applied arm blocks are the palm-heel block, bent wrist block, knife-hand block, and punching block. The foot block can also be made in many ways: the leg block which stops the opponent's kicking leg with the lower part of the leg, and kicking blocks such as the crescent kick, instep-crescent kick, stamp kick, rising side kick, and other similar kicks. In this part, only the basic arm block is covered in detail. Some of the applied arm blocks are touched upon briefly, and the remaining blocking techniques will be studied under their respective headings in later sections.

For a perfect defense in free fighting, you must combine both defensive and offensive moves advantageously, because it is difficult to stop a continuous offense with a defensive move alone. Your defensive move combined with your counterattack can easily stop the opponent from succeeding with his continuous attacks and put him into a defensive position. However, there are defensive moves other than just blocking techniques. Some of the important ways of defending in karate free fighting are stepping, shifting, smothering, jumping, instant counterattacking, guarding, and combinations of many defensive moves, all of which are studied separately in later sections.

The arm block is usually executed by striking or deflecting the opponent's attacking hand or leg. The arm block is the most vital part of the karate defensive move, and it can be successfully applied in most free-fighting situations. A strong- and well-focused arm block can not only thwart the opponent's attack but may also ruin his balance. A good arm block is usually executed at close range which puts you in a position where little adjustment for distance is necessary for your counter moves, and, furthermore, after being blocked, the opponent's position becomes weakened for following moves.

The arm block is primarily made with either the outer or inner surface of the forearm. When the arm block is made to protect the lower section of the body, it is called "low block," the middle section, "middle block," and the high section, "high block." There are several ways of delivering the arm blocks to protect each section.

9 Arm Block *(Pahl Makgi)*

● **Low Block (*Hah-dan Makgi*)**

The low block is generally practiced in three ways: the outward low block, the downward low block, and the inward low block. The inward low block will be explained later in Part IV.

Outward Low Block. This is a low block executed with the outer surface of the forearm to deflect kicks and punches which are delivered toward the lower section of the defender's body. The blocking arm travels from inside of the body toward the outside, covering the front-facing area, although its force moves in an arc pressing the arm downward first. This type of block is often performed in a front-facing posture with a twisting motion of the body, and it leads the blocker into a strong, advancing position for his counterattack. A well-focused outward low block can deflect the attacker's kicking leg so effectively that he is thrown off balance and unable to follow with combination attacks.

To make an outward low block in natural stance, raise your left arm with the fist a couple of inches over the upper portion of your right arm, palm facing inward. Then press the arm slightly downward, at the same time moving it toward the left side of your body. The blocking arm begins to turn when the block is half completed and stops directly over the left thigh with the palm facing inward. The left elbow remains very slightly bent and the distance between the fist and the thigh should be about two fist lengths. Your right fist is cocked at your waist with the shoulder tensed backward as the block is executed.

Downward Low Block. This block is performed in the same manner as the outward low block. The direction of the blocking force is primarily downward, covering the area from the solar plexus to the lower part of the body. It is preferably performed either in a half-front facing or side-facing posture. The blocker's front-facing area is blocked by the long downward blocking motion of the arm.

To make the downward low block in natural stance, bring the left arm somewhere between your right shoulder and cheek, with the palm facing the cheek. Your whole body is relaxed and your chest is open. Then, bring the blocking arm downward in a narrow circular motion to the left. The arm stops directly over the left thigh with the palm inward and the body in an approximate half-front facing posture.

Low Block in Simple Stepping. The low block can be practiced and applied with forward, back, cat, side, or any other stance.

To practice either an outward or downward low block, while stepping forward in forward stance, raise the left arm while stepping. The blocking arm is thrust downward as soon as the left foot steps down on the floor. The same procedure is applied when stepping backward.

● Middle Block (*Choong-dan Makgi*)

The middle block is an arm block performed by striking, deflecting, or pressing with the forearm against the opponent's midsection attacks. This type of block is primarily used against various hand attacks. It is also particularly effective against the roundhouse kick attack which travels in an arc parallel to the floor, rather than against kicks which rise directly from the floor. The striking area may be either the inner or outer surface of the forearm or the edge of the fist. In general, the middle block is categorized, according to the moving direction of the blocking arm, as the outward middle block or the inward middle block.

Outward Middle Block. To make an outward middle block in natural stance with the inner surface of your right arm, bring the arm across your body and place it near the left waist with the palm facing your body. The elbow is bent and the whole arm is relaxed. The other arm can be placed across the body for a reaction force while blocking. Then, raise the right fist slightly and swing the arm to the right covering the front part of the body. The forearm is twisted upward just before impact, and stops directly over the body line with the palm facing your right shoulder. The shoulder is open to about a 45-degree angle, and the elbow is bent and the upper arm is open to about a 90-degree angle. It is important that the elbow stays directly over the body line.

Outward Middle Block in Simple Stepping. As with the low block, the middle block is practiced in all the different body postures and from any stance. While stepping, the blocking arm is placed across the body and the block is executed when the forward foot touches the floor. You can also practice the block with the reverse arm.

Inward Middle Block. This is a middle block executed with the outer surface of the forearm in a reverse procedure from the outward block. The inward middle block is delivered from the outside of the body toward the inside. This is usually performed in a half-front or side-facing posture. This block is also practiced with any stance in an identical stepping procedure as the outward block.

To make an inward middle block in natural stance with your right arm, first raise the arm so the fist is approximately level with your ear, with the knuckles pointed toward the ear. The shoulder is widely open and the elbow is bent. You may place the left arm over the front part of your body to provide a reaction force by cocking it instantly to the left waist while blocking. Then, swing the right arm toward the inside of your body and stop it halfway to the left-side body line. Just before impact, twist the forearm sharply upward and at the same time pull it slightly toward you, so the palm faces your right cheek. The elbow stays inside the right-side body line, and is held closely to the body. This type of block can hardly cover the whole body area in a front-facing posture, but it can effectively cover the area from the right side to the solar-plexus area, which is the only exposed part when in a half-front or side-facing posture.

● High Block (*Sahng-Dan Makgi*)

The high block is performed by striking or deflecting with the arm the opponent's high target attacks. There are at least three types of high blocks: the outward high block, the inward high block, and the rising block. As with the middle blocks, the outward high block is made with the outer surface of the blocking arm and the inward high block with the inner surface. Both outward and inward high blocks are made and practiced in exactly the same manner as the outward and inward middle blocks, except the blocking arm in the high block swings to cover the face and other high-section areas rather than the midsection.

Rising Block (*Chookyu Makgi*). The rising block is used to protect the neck, face, and head from various hand attacks. It is made in a rising direction with the outer surface of the forearm, and is best performed in either front or half-front-facing posture from any stance.

To make a rising block in natural stance with the right arm, bring the fist directly across the body to the left side while placing the left arm in front of the body for a reaction force. The elbow is bent and the palm faces the body. Then, raise the right arm, pulling the left to a cocked position. As soon as the right arm passes your neck line, where about a foot in distance is maintained between the neck and the arm, twist the forearm so that the palm faces outward. At the same time, pull the arm toward the forehead. The block strikes the area near the

wrist, and the arm stops at a slightly higher level than your forehead with at least one fist distance between the arm and forehead. The knuckles are directly over the left side of your face, and the fist remains on a level slightly higher than the elbow.

This type of arm block deflects the attacking hand or foot. However, for a strong striking block, a rising block can be made by raising the blocking arm close to the body, passing under the other arm until the fist reaches the opposite-side shoulder line, and then it travels upward in a 45-degree forward direction with a twisting motion.

While stepping, practice the rising block in one motion. The low and middle blocks, in which the direction of blocking motion is reversed while the arm travels from the cocked to the blocking position, are performed in two units while stepping. The rising block, which also can be performed in two separate motions, can be made faster and stronger when it is completed in one motion as soon as the front foot touches the floor in forward-stance stepping.

10 Applied Arm Block

● Double-Arm Block (*Yahng-pahl Makgi*)

The double-arm block is the forearm block performed with both arms in an outward or inward direction. In the double-arm block, the actual block is made with one arm whereas the other arm follows it and is placed across the front part of the body to ensure a safe defense. This arm placement usually results in a good guard and is somewhat similar to the free-fighting position. The swinging motion of the non-blocking arm in conjunction with the actual blocking arm usually provides a strong block. It is preferably made in a half-front-facing posture with a long-distance stance which provides a strong body position. The double-arm block can be made with the knife-hand edge which will be explained in Section 12. The double-arm block can be used for either midsection or high-section defense.

Outward Double-Arm Block. To make an outward double-arm middle block in natural stance with the left forearm, bring the left arm to the right waist and at the same time extend the right arm to your right. Then, both arms swing to the left with the body-twisting motion. The block with the left arm is performed in the exact same procedure as in the outward middle block, while the right forearm moves straight to the left until it reaches the right-side body line and then blocks in with the fist near the left elbow while turning upward. The right arm remains close to the body without touching it, with the shoulder closed. The right palm faces upward.

Outward Double-Arm Low Block. To make an outward double-arm low block in natural stance with the left forearm, first bring both arms to the ready position: the left arm is placed directly over the right shoulder with the palm facing the cheek; and the right arm with its elbow bent is placed on the right side with the elbow slightly lower than shoulder level. Then, the left swings in the same manner as with the outward low block, and the right arm moves toward the solar plexus turning the palm face upward as soon as it passes the right-side body line. The right shoulder is closed and the fist remains to the left of the solar plexus. The whole block is made in a body-twisting motion.

Inward Double-Arm Low Block. To make an inward double-arm low block in back stance, first step forward and prepare for the execution of the block by placing the right arm at an approximate 45-degree angle on the right side with the palm facing straight forward, and the left fist under the right shoulder, palm facing upward. Then, swing the right arm downward and simultaneously twist the palm inward to face up as soon as it passes the right-side body line. The block is made with the outer surface of the right arm and the left arm serves mainly to guard the open area of the front body. The right arm must remain inside of the right-side body line with the elbow slightly bent.

From left: Inward double-arm low block, inward double-arm middle block, and inward double-arm high block.

● X-Block (*Kyo-Cha Makgi*)

This is an arm block performed with the crossed forearms, usually with the right over the left. It gives a strong thrusting motion and a doubly guarded arm position. Trainees sometimes apply this type of block because they have no other choice and can easily grab the attacking hand or leg to follow through with counter moves. The X-block is often practiced in a front- or half-front facing posture in forward stance, back stance, horseback-riding stance, and other similar long-distance stances. There is the upward X-block and the downward X-block. Both blocks can also be performed in the identical manner with knife-hand edges.

Upward X-Block. The upward X-block is mainly used against hand or stick attacks which are aimed at the face or head. You may effectively apply it to defend against a stamping kick attack or other attacks when lying on the floor or sitting without being prepared to guard.

To make the upward X-block in natural stance, first cross both forearms at the right ribs. Then, raise them directly toward your face stopping the cross of the arms in front of your forehead. About a foot's distance is maintained between the forehead and the crossed arms. The outer surfaces of both forearms face directly forward.

Downward X-Block. The execution of this block is identical to the upward X-block except the blocking force is thrust downward instead of upward. The downward X-block is primarily applied against the opponent's front-kick attack.

Bring both arms directly under the right shoulder and cross them with the right over the left. Thrust both arms downward toward the abdomen so that the cross of the arms stops about a foot away from it.

● Others

Circular-Motion Block (*Tollyu Makgi*). This block is performed in a circular motion by lifting and deflecting the opponent's kicking leg with the blocking arm swinging simultaneously upward and outward in a continuous motion. The block begins with an inward low block and ends with an outward middle or high block. This type of block is particularly effective against a combined front kick and punch attack, because the kicking opponent is usually rendered off balance for his punch attack when his kicking leg is lifted and deflected.

Bent Wrist Block (*Pahl-Mohk Makgi*). This block deflects the punching hand with the bent wrist in a rising motion.

Back-Hand Block (*Son-duhng Makgi*). This deflects the punching hand in an outward direction with the back part of an open hand.

Punching Block (*Chyu Makgi*). This arm block, using the outer surface, is performed in a punching motion deflecting the opponent's attacking hand and converting the blocking arm into a punch at the same time.

Palm-Heel Block (*Chang-kwon Makgi*). This block deflects the opponent's punching arm with the palm-heel in an inward direction. (Details of the palm-heel strike will be explained in Section 13.)

Pressing Block (*Noollu Makgi*). This type of block is performed with the palm-heel, bottom-fist, or forearm by pressing the attacking hand or leg downward.

Knife-Hand Edge Block (*Shooto Makgi*). This block strikes the attacking hand or leg with the knife-hand edge in an outward direction. (Details will be explained in Section 12.)

Part V Hand Techniques
(Sohn Tsugi)

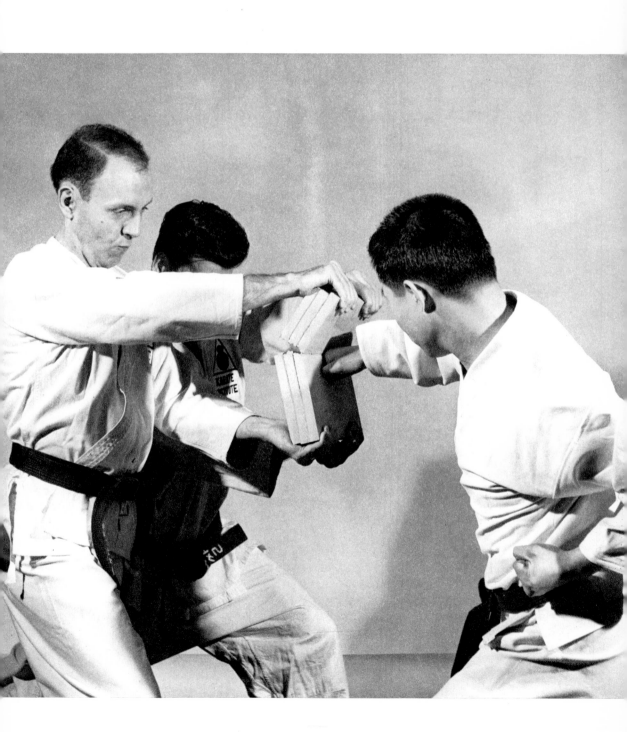

A PUNCH is any hand attack with the closed fist or knuckle that travels directly to the target; some attacks, like the hook and uppercut punches, are executed in an arc with the direct generation of power from the tightened muscles of the body. A strike is primarily made with an open hand traveling in either a vertical or horizontal arc. While the body force is not neglected in a strike, the power of the arm alone is chiefly used. Open hand attacks with the palm-heel or spear-hand, which are projected directly from the body to the target, are called simply a thrust, rather than a strike or punch.

Hand attacks which are designated as snap punches are executed swiftly, with an instantaneous contraction of all muscles on contact. The thrust punch or strike involves a gradual tensing of the muscles of the attacking arm and body, and deep penetration into the target. Involvement of the hip and shoulder in punches and strikes is the province of the advanced karate or *taekwon do* practitioner and adds range and power.

In general, hand techniques have many advantages when they are applied in free fighting. First, punching and striking techniques are easy to apply with speed and without loss of balance. Second, the hands can be quickly converted into blocks and used in more combinations than foot attacks. Third, they are located nearer to most of the opponent's vital targets, and, therefore, can reach the target faster since they have less distance to travel. A knife-hand strike to the side of the neck, for example, involves less distance than a kick to the same target. Fourth, they are relatively easy to direct accurately to the target. Fifth, many punches and strikes can be delivered continuously without extreme body maneuver. Sixth, while attacking with hand techniques, the body balance can be strongly retained, because the weight is on both feet rather than one foot as when delivering a kick.

Some disadvantages occur when hand techniques are applied in free fighting. When employing a hand technique, an opening for counterattack is created because half of the body is deprived of its natural guard. Another disadvantage is that the techniques are applied at a close distance and therefore create equal danger from an opponent's response while moving into his range. A kick, on the other hand, can be executed from a safer distance.

11 Straight Fist Punch (*Chung-Kwon Chigi*)

● **How to Make the Straight Fist Punch**

Making the Fist. Assuming the natural stance, you extend your arms before you, palm facing outward. The fingers of the hands are bent at the first joint with their tips pressed against the third joint as tightly as possible. The fist is then made by folding over the fingers again into the palm. The thumbs are tucked tightly underneath the fist, for the striking point is the face of the first two knuckles. The striking front of the hand should be flat and square, and the wrist straight with the arm bone backing the first two fingers. Without a strong fist, blows will be ineffective and the practitioner will hurt his own fingers or wrist upon striking a hard object.

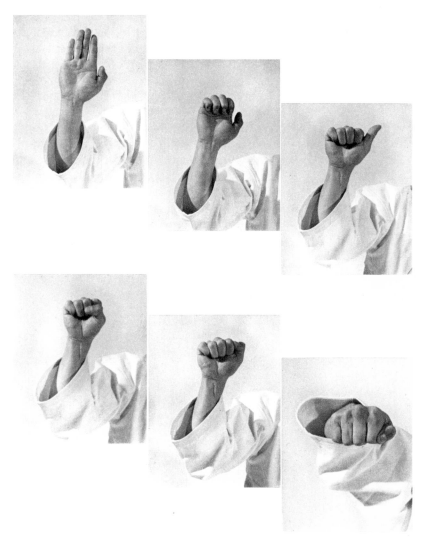

Throwing the Straight Fist Punch. The straight fist punch is always aimed at a real or imaginary target at a set distance away. At the point of impact, the muscles of the body contract, which in combination with the speed of the blow, the twisting power of the forearm, and the withdrawing force of the opposite arm, give maximum power. The elbows are kept slightly bent and not locked at the point of impact.

In natural stance, cock your fists on your hip, thumb upward, ready to punch, but relax your shoulders. The fist is thrust straight forward, palm upward, halfway to the imaginary target; then the wrist begins to twist. At the point of impact, the forearm is fully twisted so the palm points downward, and the bottom knuckles of the first two fingers strike the target. In making the second punch, the forward hand is withdrawn as the rear hand is extended with an equal expenditure of energy to provide a natural reaction force. Both hands should be exchanged simultaneously.

Thrusting Power. In order to make a forceful thrusting straight fist punch, deliver it after cocking your hip and shoulder slightly back, making sure that the fist travels in a direct line to its target as shown in the picture below. While punching, avoid the mistake of throwing your shoulder toward the opponent as a boxer does, for it endangers the balance and coordination. The shoulder always remains relaxed both before and after the punch is thrown and it should be tensed momentarily only at impact.

A straight fist punch can be performed without twisting the arm by thrusting it out from a cocked position where the fist is held with the thumb upward.

● Practice of the Straight Fist Punch

A straight fist punch, as with any other hand technique, can be practiced in any karate stance from a stationary position, or while stepping, turning, twisting, or extending the front foot to move into another stance. The reverse fist punch as well as the forward punch, double, or triple fist punches, or combinations with other hand, foot, and blocking techniques are also practiced for high, middle, and low sections of the body.

In Stationary Stance. To make a straight fist punch in horseback-riding stance, first cock both fists over the hips but do not extend them past the body. Both palms face upward and the chest is widely open. Then, thrust the left fist forward to an imaginary target in front of you at the height of your own solar-plexus and the center of your body line. Avoid the common mistake of bending your wrist.

In Simple Stepping. While stepping forward or backward in forward stance, you can practice a forward fist punch which is made with the left fist when the left leg is forward in forward stance, as well as a reverse punch. To practice a forward punch while stepping forward, deliver the punch with the cocked fist with a slight twist of the body at the last moment as the forward foot returns to the floor into a new spot, simultaneously cocking the other fist back for a reaction force. Your stepping is made smoothly with the body posture facing straight forward and upward if the punch is practiced in a front-facing posture, with your rear hip usually being pushed forward as soon as the step is completed.

For a stronger straight fist punch, you can lean your body slightly to the side while stepping, so the fist which has already punched remains in forward direction and the waist at which the cocked fist is held remains far backward. As soon as the step is completed, the punch is delivered while twisting the body forward and straightening the rear knee. This method is good for a thrust punch and is often practiced with the reverse punch. A straight fist punch is called a side punch when it is delivered to your side in side stance.

You can practice the straight fist punch while stepping in side stance. While adjusting for distance in straight stepping and rotating your body in pivot stepping, you cock your punching fist at the waist and deliver it with a slight body twist as soon as the step is completed. Your body remains upright and the chest is widely open with your head turned to the side to face the target directly.

Extending the Front Foot. In order to make a reverse straight fist punch in free fighting from a short distance, shift your body weight toward the target by extending the front foot slightly forward into forward or low stance. Simultaneously deliver the fist punch while twisting your upper body slightly forward. Either hand is used to make the punch. To use the forward fist punch, cock it first at the side of the body line and thrust it out instantaneously while shifting.

This type of punching move is accompanied by the extension of the front foot and often by deflecting the opponent's front-guarding arm. To cover extra distance while extending the front foot forward, you can begin the attacking move with a spot shift, which is made by moving both feet forward simultaneously in a quick hopping motion.

● How to Use the Straight Fist Punch

The straight fist punch can be used against almost any target, such as solar plexus, ribs, kidney, groin, face, and throat, but in practice try to aim mainly for the solar plexus to avoid accidents. Anyone who can constantly score in training upon an opponent's solar plexus, which is the most easily guarded area of the body, can shift to a more open target if the occasion for self-defense arises. However, the midsection area around the whole body should be considered the main striking area for the straight fist punch.

The straight fist punch is an effective blow preferred by many free fighters. It is applied from any free-fighting stance for an initial attack, either alone or in combination with other blows. While delivering the fist punch, you must guard your front-facing area with the other arm. In general, the straight fist punch is effective in combination with kicks, which will be explained in later sections. A punch must be delivered distinctively for it to be a point in free fighting.

When the distance between you and your opponent is close enough, you can use the straight fist punch from a static position or by simply moving forward with the weight shift into a longer-distance stance. The punch is accompanied by a simple form of stepping when the distance is great. Adjustment for distance is frequently used to make the whole body movement effective and the punch reach the target aimed at.

Adjustment for Distance. When a punch is to be made with the rear fist at a long distance from your opponent, you can initiate your attacking move with an adjustment for distance by extending the front foot forward just prior to the simple step which accompanies the punch. A second adjustment for distance is made by bringing the rear foot forward and placing it at an appropriate spot at the right distance from the target to deliver the punch with the front fist or with the rear fist for a reverse punch. The adjustment for distance can be effectively applied when the opponent defends by shifting backward.

In order to make a straight fist punch with your right fist, cock it while adjusting for distance. The distance covered by your rear foot is as long as necessary depending upon how

far back your opponent is expected to move. While adjusting and cocking the right fist, make sure you guard your front-facing area with the other hand to protect against an instant counterattack. Your punch is delivered simultaneously with the extension of your front foot forward.

Deflecting the Guarding Arm. It is generally to be expected that free fighters are always in a guarded position with arms ready for blocking. As the arms are apt to be tense at the point of their opponents' attacks, they are very sensitive to unexpected deflection. The deflection of an opponent's front-guarding arm usually accompanies an adjustment for distance or a successful punching attack, for it instantaneously upsets the opponent's carefully conceived defensive plan. Even the simple act of deflecting the opponent's front-guarding arm gives an idea of how he will move and his reaction to the attacker's initial move. In any case, you can frequently create an opening directly under the arm by knocking it away.

Simple Stepping Inward. This section covers the initial straight fist punch executed from the usual free-fighting position by stepping forward, on contact, into a new spot at the inward side of the opponent's front foot. The most opportune time to apply a straight fist punch is when you are in a front- or half-front facing posture toward your opponent. Whether the position is same-side facing or opposite-side facing, the procedure of stepping forward to punch is identical.

Adjust for distance by moving either the front or the rear foot, depending upon your starting position, and simultaneously attack with a straight fist punch. Cock your punching fist while adjusting for distance, especially in the case of an opposite-side facing position. Since the forward part of your body is open to counterattack, you must prepare for guarding while stepping. Continue with a series of combination attacks if your initial punch is blocked, or break off your attack with a block and/or shift away to a safe position if the opponent replies with an instant counterattack. However, any stepping and punching moves should be done in one fast single unit action.

Simple Stepping Outward. When an opponent is in a side-facing posture or his main vital area is not directly open to you, so that your straight-fist-punch attack in an inward stepping move will not be effective, you can step forward placing your front foot on the outside of his and attack his rib cage with a straight fist punch. This method of moving forward is almost the same as the inward stepping move, except you are attacking at an angle outside his front foot. Your straight fist punch must be delivered with the advancing force of your body. Even if the initial punching attack does not score on your opponent, the strong advancing motion will force him into an unbalanced position so that you may proceed with other attacks or destroy his possibilities for counterattacking and return to a safe position. However, once you get into the new spot, you leave very little opening for his counterattack. Execute a straight fist punch as soon as you step into forward or low stance to the outside of the opponent, causing him to move to protect himself and thus weakening his balance. Then you can punch or use a variety of attacks when he seeks to regain his stance. Remember that you will be in an awkward position unless your advancing force is strong enough to throw your opponent off balance. While moving in, deflect the opponent's front-guarding arm if it is in your way. Whether you attack from a same-side or an opposite-side-facing position, execute the moves as a single unit in full speed, following an adjustment for distance if it is required.

Moving into a Side-Facing Posture. A straight fist punch can be effectively applied in side stance or in a side-facing posture from any stance, providing the target is facing directly on your side. Such a fist punch can be delivered as an initial attack or as a combination attack following through on the opponent who defends with open shifting. While delivering the punch in a side-facing posture, your body is less open to counterattack than with a front- or half-front facing posture.

Your straight fist punch can be applied from an oblique direction following an adjustment for distance. While you are bringing your rear foot forward and your opponent responds to it, expecting your forward fist punch, you may change your moving direction slightly to your left side and execute a side punch.

In Jumping Motion. A straight fist punch can be delivered with either the front or rear fist accompanied by a jumping motion. This type of move instantly shortens the free-fighting distance by pushing your body forward in the air toward your opponent, either with both feet simultaneously, or with the front or rear foot. In both instances, your guarding arm must be placed to cover your body while jumping, and the front leg should be cocked upward at the last moment to protect your front-facing area from your opponent's counter moves.

To make a straight fist punch with your right fist in a jumping motion, push your body forward in the air toward the opponent with your left leg, simultaneously rotating your body slightly to the left. While jumping, your left arm is carefully placed to guard and the right knee is slightly raised as soon as your body rotates to protect your front-facing area from the opponent's instant counterattack. The punching fist is cocked while jumping, and is usually delivered from the air.

Straight Fist Punch Following a Faking Move. Execute a faking move to mislead your opponent and create an opening for a following punch. The faking move must be made without full force behind it so the following punch can be fully coordinated with the fake and catch the opponent totally off guard.

Sometimes the faking move is performed in a manner similar to the deflection move. A fake punch with either arm can be accompanied by an adjustment for distance, a step, or it can be made from a stationary position in order to follow with an appropriate step and punch while the defending opponent shifts away. A straight fist punch is usually best combined with a fake kick, but it can sometimes score following a fake move with the hands.

To surprise the opponent with a reverse straight middle punch with the right fist in a same-side-facing position, you can first fake with your left hand following an adjustment for distance. Both of your arms must be in a guarding position to protect yourself against a potential instant counterattack while adjusting. The opponent who habitually plans to counterattack following a short arm block against your forward fist can sometimes be scored against if you make a short fake punch with your left hand while extending your left foot forward and then simultaneously follow through, moving into forward or low stance and executing a right fist punch. Both hand moves must be made as a single unit.

● Defense Against the Straight Fist Punch

In defense against the straight fist punch attack in free fighting, a single fist punch can be arm blocked easily. Combination punches should be avoided by body shifting. A side-facing posture leaves virtually no opening on the front part of your body for the attacking opponent's straight fist punch, which is delivered directly toward you. Therefore, the area you must guard is relatively limited. Since the attacker often leaves his midsection area widely open while delivering a straight fist punch, an instant counterattack frequently scores effectively. However, in this section, only defenses against simple methods of straight-fist-punching attacks are covered. The defense against the straight fist punch in combination with other hand or foot attacks will be covered in later sections.

Arm Block Against a Single Straight Fist Punch. Against a single straight fist punch, whether it is a forward or reverse punch, you can defend with an arm block or a double-arm block, either inward, outward, rising, or downward depending upon the target to be guarded. The block is often made with the front-guarding arm. In the picture to the left, as soon as the inward middle block is completed it is necessary to prepare at once to guard your front-facing kidneys against a possible reverse punch attack. You might counterattack with a reverse punch following your arm block.

Straight Counter Fist Punch Following an Arm Block. Either a forward or reverse straight punch can follow a successful arm block. The arm block is often accompanied by body shifting, and correct body posture plays an important role in defense against the straight-fist-punch attack. It is most important that the block and counterpunch be executed quickly so the attacking opponent is not able to prepare a defense against it.

To make a safer defense against a straight fist punch, you can combine your arm block with simple backward shifting in a side-facing posture. While shifting, do not swing your body, but rather rotate the entire body to move it backward, maintaining a tight guard for your front-facing area. You can make a quick counterattack with a straight reverse punch following the complete defensive move. Your counterattacking fist should be cocked automatically as you make the inward middle block.

Straight Counter Fist Punch Following Body Shifting. This move consists of a straight counter punch accompanied by spot shifting against a straight-fist-punch attack. This is called counter shifting because both the offensive and defensive moves are made with body shifting. Many ways of counter shifting can be combined, applying the most suitable body-shifting moves to each different defensive situation. Some of the counter-shifting practices will be explained in greater detail in the later sections on kicks.

Successful defense can be accomplished by open stepping, which is performed by spot shifting as the attacking opponent delivers a straight fist punch. Your feet should be relatively close together in order to make an agile move. At the same time, tightly guard your front-facing area. Then you can deliver a straight counter punch, accompanied by simple body shifting, before the opponent regains his coordination following his initial attack.

Instant Counter Punch. Instant counterattacking means a counterattack which is delivered against the attacking opponent as soon as he begins to initiate his attack. You can apply many kicks as instant counterattacks against the straight fist punch, using your arms to guard while kicking, because kicks reach farther than a punch. Usually you can make a successful instant counter punch if you detect the type of attack the opponent is going to make before he executes it. When you detect him beginning to move toward you to make a straight punching attack, you can simultaneously move slightly toward him and deliver your punch first, either in forward or side stance, using your other hand to deflect his punch. Since this is a matter of your punching attack against your opponent's punching attack, the whole move must be made at full speed. However, you may score more effectively by delivering such an instant attack while moving forward in a slightly sideway direction. The instant counter punch generally should not be applied too often in free fighting.

As your opponent begins to step to deliver his straight fist punch, you can extend your front foot 45 degrees forward and simultaneously deliver a side punch. The entire counter move must be made instantly, otherwise you will be in an awkward position to guard against the opponent's potential combination attacks. Even if your punch scores, you must move into a well-guarded position at once.

12 Knife-Hand Strike
(Shooto Chigi)

THE KNIFE-HAND strike is a blow delivered with the outer edge of the hand. It can be a strong and effective blow when executed correctly, with the main force of the body directly related to it. Since the striking edge of the hand is narrow, the striking blow can deliver a concentrated force to a small area causing substantial damage. The trainee must always keep in mind that, while performing this movement, his elbow joint must remain slightly bent, so the shock of impact is not transmitted to the joint. This blow is generally used to attack the head, face, neck, throat, collarbone, chest, ribs, kidneys, and body joints. The striking hand is usually cocked over the shoulder, and it travels either parallel to the floor or downward, depending upon the height of the target.

● How to Make the Knife-Hand Strike

Making the Knife-Hand Edge. The knife-hand is made by opening the hand widely with the four fingers held closely together. Tuck the thumb down and press it backward with tension and simultaneously extend the little finger straight with equal tension. Slightly bend the first and second joints of the remaining three fingers. The whole hand should be very tense, and the striking surface is the entire area circled in the above picture. The wrist should be bent slightly outward and upward in order to avoid striking with the little finger joint. The small bone under the wrist joint can be effectively used on weak targets.

Inward Strike. This is a blow performed in an outward-inward arc in order to strike the target from the side. The striking hand is brought up to a position over the shoulder, slightly behind the ear. The chest and shoulders are open and the elbow is tightly bent; the wrist is slightly bent so the palm faces somewhat upward. Then, the hand is swung inward in a wide arc with a snapping motion. At impact, the palm should face upward, the elbow remaining slightly bent, and the hand in front of the body.

Outward Strike. Raise the striking hand to a position over the opposite shoulder, near the ear, with the palm facing the cheek. Then, swing it outward in a wide arc, traveling parallel to the floor to strike an imaginary target at neck height. The hand should be twisted at the point of impact so the palm faces downward. The hand must be stopped at the body line with the elbow slightly bent.

Downward Strike. This blow is delivered in a wide downward arc, mainly against the top of the head or shoulders. The blow is executed in a manner similar to the inward strike, except that the arc is vertical rather than horizontal.

Raise your striking hand over the shoulder, behind the ear in the same way as with the inward strike. Your shoulders are open and the elbow is tightly bent, raised slightly higher than for the inward strike. Then, swing your arm downward in a vertical arc with a snapping motion, stopping the hand in the center of the body line with the elbow remaining slightly bent.

The downward strike can often be made in a descending curve from either the inward or outward cocked position to strike a target such as the collarbone.

● Knife-Hand as a Block

Knife-Hand Block. The knife-hand block usually means an outward middle block striking with the knife-hand edge, with the other hand placed in front of the solar plexus. The blocking hand is swung in the same manner as the strike, but usually from a half-front or side-facing posture. It is generally made with the hand on the same side as the advanced foot when practiced from mobile stances.

To make a knife-hand block in natural stance with your left hand, raise it over your right shoulder with the palm facing the ear while the right arm remains extended. Then, swing the left arm outward in a descending curve, simultaneously withdrawing the other hand toward your solar plexus. At the last moment, twist the left hand outward so the palm faces almost down, and the right hand inward with the palm up. The left hand and elbow, which is slightly bent, stop over the body line, with the shoulder slightly open.

Double Knife-Hand Block. The double knife-hand block is made by swinging both hands in an arc. This block is made in the same way as the double arm block, and the positions of the hands and body are exactly the same as the knife-hand block previously covered.

To make the block with the right hand, bring it over the left shoulder. Keep the left hand on your left side (the palm facing downward and the shoulders closed). Then, swing the right hand in the same way as the single knife-hand block, simultaneously pulling the left hand toward the solar plexus in an arc, traveling parallel to the floor.

Others. Most of the arm blocks can be replaced by the knife-hand block: an inward middle knife-hand block *(top photo)*, an outward low knife-hand block *(middle photo)*, or a rising knife-hand block *(right bottom photo)*.

● How to Use the Knife-Hand Strike

The application of the knife-hand strike in free fighting is identical to the straight fist punch in terms of the body positions, adjustment for distance, and foot moves. The blow should be aimed at a target which is open in a sideway or downward direction. Furthermore, it is preferable to any other type of blow for targets such as the cheeks and neck, because the narrow edge of the striking hand can reach the target without hitting other spots first. The knife-hand strike is frequently applied in free fighting in combination with other hand and/or foot techniques. A few examples are cited to give the trainee a general idea of its application.

In Simple Stepping. In order to deliver an inward knife-hand strike with your rear hand, cock your hand while making a simple step. Be sure to guard your front-facing area with the other hand as you initiate the step to protect yourself against the opponent's potential instant counterattack. Instead, you can deflect his arm, momentarily surprising him, and deliver the strike to his neck as soon as the step is completed. The simple step is frequently followed by an adjustment for distance.

In a Jumping Motion. A downward knife-hand strike can be effectively applied in a jumping motion toward the opponent. The jumping move is accompanied by any necessary adjustment for distance. The strike is delivered from the air. As you jump, guard your front-facing area with your other hand and raise the rear knee slightly to guard against an instant counterattack. The raised knee also acts as a fake, attracting the opponent's attention, as you cock and strike with your rear hand. When you do not have sufficient height to strike his head, the blow can be delivered to a lower target such as his shoulder. (An outward strike can also be applied instead.)

13 Other Attacks

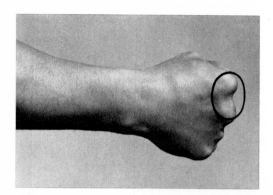

● **Back-Fist Punch (*Choo Muk-dung Chigi*)**

This is a blow which utilizes the back of the fist, delivered with a snapping motion of the arm. The targets are the head, face, temple, chin, chest, solar plexus, ribs, kidneys, and the back. The elbow must always remain slightly bent, otherwise the elbow joint can be injured because of the snapping motion. The back-fist punch is usually made in three ways: downward, outward, and curving upward.

Downward Punch. In order to practice a downward back-fist punch with your right fist while stepping forward, cock it directly behind the right-side ear with the palm facing forward and the shoulders widely open. As soon as the right foot returns to the floor in a new stance, the punch is completed by delivering it in a vertical arc traveling directly over the ear. The arm is twisted at the last moment so the back of the fist faces downward. The downward back-fist punch is often practiced in side stance.

While stepping, cock the right fist in front of your left chest with the palm facing downward. The punch should be delivered in a vertical arc passing over your left ear to the right, with snapping motion, and twisting the fist at the last moment so the palm faces upward.

Outward Punch. To practice an outward back-fist punch with the right fist while stepping in side stance, cock the right fist directly over the left chest with the palm facing downward. Then swing it in a horizontal arc to the right, with a snapping motion, twisting the fist at the last moment so the palm faces forward. The blow should be completed as soon as the right foot returns to the floor in side stance, and the arm stays directly over the body line.

Rising-Curve Punch. In order to make a rising-curve punch with your right fist, cock the right fist in front of your left rib cage with the palm facing downward. Then, swing it upward and simultaneously to your right, with a snapping motion, twisting the fist at the last minute so the palm faces to the left. The arm stays directly over your right-side body line.

When to Use the Back-Fist Punch. The back-fist punch is frequently applied in free fighting when you and your opponent are close together. It is also used as a counter punch following an arm block with the same-side fist. Moreover, it frequently scores effectively when used as a second attack following kicks.

In order to deliver an outward back-fist punch in a same-side facing position, adjust for distance, first bringing the rear foot forward. Then, jump toward the opponent by extending the front foot forward into side stance, and simultaneously deliver the punch as a surprise attack. This blow can be effective but is somewhat lacking in power or coordination.

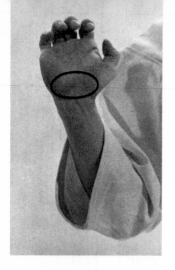

● Palm-Heel Attack (*Chang-kwon Chigi*)

This is a blow made with the heel of the palm, either as a thrust in a straight forward direction or as a strike in a vertical or horizontal arc. This blow is primarily used for attacking but is also frequently used as a block to deflect the attacking opponent's arm or leg in an upward, downward, or inward direction. As with other forms of hand attacks, the palm-heel attack can be a highly effective blow providing it is delivered from the correct distance with proper timing. Some of the targets for the palm-heel attack are the head, face, temple, chin, solar plexus, rib cage, floating ribs, and kidneys. This attack is generally practiced in four different ways; forward, upward, downward, and hooking.

Forward Thrust. In order to make a forward palm-heel thrust with your right hand, first cock the heel of the palm at your right waist. Then, thrust it straight forward with the palm facing forward and the outer edge of the hand pointing downward. To attack a high target such as the face or chin, you can twist your arm inward while thrusting it so the outer edge of your hand faces to the right.

Upward Strike. To practice an upward palm-heel strike with the right hand in forward stance, cock the right hand while stepping by placing it at an angle behind the right kidney. Then, swing it upward in a vertical arc toward an imaginary target directly in front of your chest as the right foot returns to the floor in forward stance. Twist the arm upward so the palm faces up at the point of impact. The elbow should be quite bent and the shoulders open. This type of blow often scores as an uppercut strike.

Downward Strike. To make a downward palm-heel strike with the right hand, cock it by bringing it directly over your right shoulder with the palm facing upward. Then, swinging the arm in a vertical arc, strike an imaginary target directly in front of your face. The elbow should be slightly bent. This type of strike also can be made in a descending curve when the situation arises.

Hooking Strike. In order to practice a hooking palm-heel strike in side stance, cock the left hand at a backward angle, with the elbow bent and the shoulders tightly closed. Then, swing it inward in a horizontal arc, hooking it at the last moment so the palm faces forward and the elbow is bent. This type of strike should be practiced in all the different karate stances.

How to Use the Palm-Heel Attack. The palm-heel attack is primarily used close to your opponent in free fighting. It is frequently used in combination moves following kicks or other hand attacks. The upward, downward, and hooking strikes cannot easily be defended against by simple arm blocks, especially when the block is aimed at the midsection of the striking arm, for the arm travels in an arc with the elbow bent, and can sometimes still strike the target even if the block hits the arm. However, the palm-heel attack can be applied in free fighting as an initial attack and is generally delivered with a pushing motion.

In this use of the palm-heel attack in free fighting, you can deliver a hooking strike effectively while stepping. In order to initiate the attack, you should deflect the opponent's front-guarding arm with your front arm while making any necessary adjustment for distance. Use the front arm to guard your front-facing area while cocking your rear hand and making a simple step. The hooking strike is completed as soon as your rear foot returns to the floor outside of the opponent's front leg.

● Elbow Attack (*Pahl-koom-chi Chigi*)

This blow strikes with the elbow in a thrusting motion. It is a strong and effective blow when applied at a close distance. The striking targets are the head, face, chin, solar plexus, ribs, kidneys, and many spots on the back of the body. The elbow attack is delivered in five ways: inward, outward, upward, downward, and backward.

Inward Attack. Bend the right elbow tightly and cock it by bringing it backward with the palm facing upward with your body in a half-front-facing posture. Then, swing it forward and inward in a narrow horizontal arc, simultaneously twisting the right side of the body slightly forward. The point of the elbow stops in front of the right side of the chest, with the arm twisted inward at the last moment so the palm faces down. While striking, keep the elbow tightly bent and the fist downward in order to avoid hitting your face with your own fist.

Outward Attack. To make an outward elbow attack with the right elbow, cock it by bringing it directly in front of the chest with the fist over the left shoulder and the palm facing the cheek. Your body is twisted slightly to the left side. Then, swing it outward in a narrow horizontal arc toward an imaginary target on the right side. While striking, your body straightens, adding force, and the elbow stops directly at your right side with the palm facing downward.

Upward Attack. Cock the right elbow by bringing it all the way back with the palm facing inward. You are in a half-front facing posture with your right side slightly back. Then, swing the elbow upward in a narrow vertical arc toward an imaginary target directly in front of your face. The elbow is tightly bent with the fist directly over the right shoulder and the palm facing downward. While swinging, drive the elbow slightly inward, being careful to avoid hitting your face with your own fist.

Downward Attack. Cock the right elbow by raising it on your right side with the fist directly behind the head and the palm facing forward. Then, swing it forward and downward in a narrow vertical arc, striking an imaginary target directly in front of your right side, with the palm facing inward. The body is twisted slightly back on the right side while the elbow is cocked, and twists forward simultaneously with the attack in order to provide a longer reach.

Backward Attack. Cock the right elbow by placing the arm across the front part of the body, with the fist directly over the left shoulder and the palm facing downward. Your right side is twisted slightly forward, and you look back over your right shoulder. Then, swing the elbow to the right and backward as you twist your right side slightly backward. The fist is tightly closed, pointing slightly inward and the palm faces up.

● Miscellaneous Attacks

Spear-Hand Thrust (*Kwan-soo Tzirugi*). This blow strikes with the tips of the three middle fingers which are held tightly together with the ends even. The spear-hand is made in the same way as the knife-hand. This blow is primarily delivered in a straight forward direction as with the straight fist punch. The targets are the eyes, throat, solar plexus, floating ribs, and kidneys. The use of this blow in free fighting is very limited, since it is intended to attack weak, vulnerable spots and could cause serious injury. However, it can be a valuable self-defense technique.

In order to practice a spear-hand thrust with the right hand in natural stance, cock the hand on your right side with the palm facing upward. Then, thrust it forward toward an imaginary target directly in front of your solar plexus, by first raising the hand slightly and twisting inward so the palm faces the left. At the same time, the other hand is pulled toward the body, stopping directly under the right elbow with the left palm facing downward. For a target such as the eyes, the right hand can be twisted so the palm faces downward, or it can be delivered with the palm up against a target such as the throat.

Uppercut Punch (*Coohkyu Chigi*). This blow strikes with the fore-fist in an upward arc without the full extension of the arm. The punching power is directly transmitted from the body while the elbow is quite bent and held close to the body. The targets are the chin, solar plexus, ribs, and kidneys. This blow is only delivered from a short distance and provides a strong attack.

Hook Punch (*Tohllyu Chigi*). This blow is delivered in a narrow horizontal arc, striking with the fore-fist, without the full extension of the arm. The punching fist thrusts forward first until the elbow passes the waist and then hooks inward, striking an imaginary target from the side. The power is directly transmitted from the body as with the uppercut punch. This blow is also used at close range and the targets are the face, chin, solar plexus, ribs, and kidneys.

Bottom-Fist Punch (*Choomuk-pahdak Chigi*). This is a blow which utilizes the bottom of the fist, usually striking in a downward arc. Sometimes, it strikes outward in the same way as the back-fist punch. This is a strong blow, particularly effective against the head, temple, collarbone, and base of the neck.

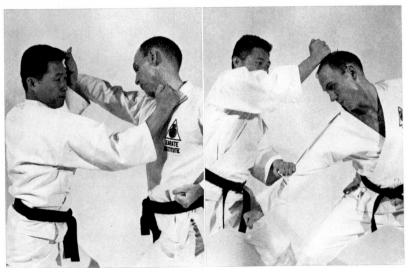

Knuckle Punch (*Kwan-chul Chigi*). This blow strikes with the knuckles which are formed in various ways. It is a very weak move and should be used only against weak spots such as eyes, temple, throat, bridge of the nose, and kidneys.

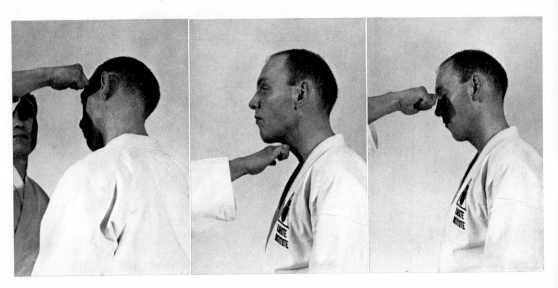

Inner-Edge Strike (*Yukto Chigi*). This blow strikes with the inner-edge of the hand, primarily in a horizontal arc. This is performed in the same way as the inward and outward knife-hand strikes, except the opposite edge of the hand is used. The targets are weak spots such as eyes, bridge of the nose, chin, temple, and throat.

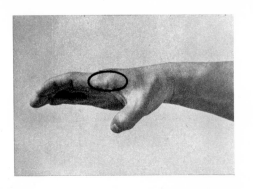

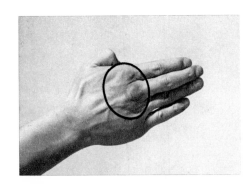

Back-Hand Strike (*Son-dung Chigi*). This blow strikes with the back of the hand, primarily in an outward direction. It is performed in the same manner as the outward back-fist punch. This is a very weak blow. It can be used as a block, deflecting an attacking hand. Targets are the ears, eyes, and groin.

Part VI Front Kick Moves
(Ahp Chagi)

14 How to Make the Front Kick

THE FRONT kick is easy to learn and hard to perfect. You can easily combine many techniques with a front-kick attack in free fighting, because its execution allows you to retain good balance. With a front kick you can attack most of the vital points of the body such as the groin, ribs, armpit, chest, solar plexus, and head.

The front kick can be executed in the following ways: front limbering-up kick, front snap kick, front thrust kick, front-pushing kick, and flying front kick. The ball of the foot is the striking surface for all the front kicks except the pushing kick where the flat of the foot is used.

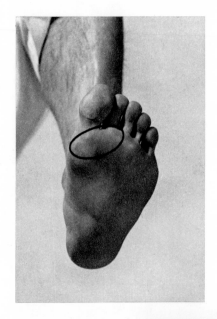

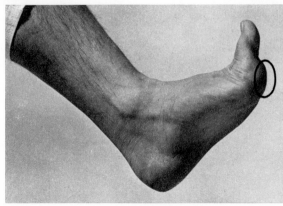

● Front-Limbering-Up Kick (*Ahp Ohlligi*)

The front-limbering-up kick stretches the muscles under the knee and thigh and loosens the joints so the snap and thrust kicks can be performed smoothly and effectively. It enables you to perform a high snap kick from a balanced position. It is an important exercise that should be repeated in every class, as well as in practice sessions outside of class.

The front-limbering-up kick is often made with the rear foot from forward or back stance. Bring your rear foot forward and, as soon as it passes your front foot, straighten the knee of your kicking leg and swing it up as high as possible in an arc toward your body, attempting (but not succeeding) to touch your face with the shin bone. Your ankle is flexed back to its full length for added strength. Your upper body is erect or even bent a bit forward, and your supporting knee is slightly bent to provide good balance. Never lean backward or you may fall.

● Front Snap Kick (*Ahp Cha-pusugi*)

The knee plays a very important role in the delivery of the front snap kick. This kick is not used as a finishing technique, but rather as a fast attack with a shocking impact. You must retain a perfect balance after its execution, with the toe of your supporting foot facing straight toward the opponent. Because good balance can be maintained easily after making the kick, this type of kick is best used in combination attacks.

Assuming forward stance, curl up the toes of your rear foot, and flex your ankle slightly. Simultaneously, raise your knee so the upper leg is parallel with the floor. Your lower leg should be cocked backward toward the thigh. The kick is executed with a snapping motion of your knee while raising the thigh slightly. The kicking foot is then brought back to the cocked position and lowered to the floor. The delivery of the kick and the return of the kicking foot to the originally cocked position must both be performed in one continuous snapping motion. This prevents the opponent from catching the foot, and puts you in a ready position for the next move. The power of the kick is focused at the point of impact. The supporting knee should be slightly bent and body posture should be straight to maintain good balance. Do not jerk your body while kicking but make the whole move in a simple and smooth motion.

● Front Thrust Kick (*Ahp Cha-tzirugi*)

The front thrust kick is often used to reach a distant target as one advances toward the opponent. It is an extremely strong kick, used as a finishing attack in free-fighting matches. However, the kicking leg can be easily blocked or caught because the body advancement involved while delivering the kick transfers the entire body weight forward and it is hard to cock back the kicking leg to the body line following the execution of the kick. Therefore, a combination move, especially with hand attacks should often be used.

Assuming forward stance, raise your rear knee with the lower part of your leg cocked as in the front snap kick. Before delivering the kick, bring your knee as high as possible toward your chest while flexing the ankle upward. Simultaneously thrust the foot forward to the target in a slightly rising direction, whipping the ball of the foot forward. Push your hip slightly forward with the power of your whole body, tensing at the beginning of the delivery and gradually increasing the tension as the foot moves toward the target. After the completion of the kick, pull the kicking leg back to the cocked position and step forward. The toes of your supporting foot should be slightly open, facing at an angle to the direction of your body movement in order to allow your kicking side to lean slightly forward with the kick but maintain good balance.

● Front-Pushing Kick (*Ahp Cha-meelgi*)

This kick is designed to push an opponent away, or to propel yourself away from a smothered or held position. The striking surface is usually the flat of the foot, but the ball or heel can also be used.

Assuming back stance, bring your front knee directly to your chest, raising the flat of your foot till it is almost pointing at the target. Then thrust it forward in a straight line. Your upper body should lean back slightly to keep the pushing leg level. When you pull your kicking leg back to the cocked position, your upper body simultaneously moves forward on your supporting leg.

● Flying Front Kick (*Dtuiyu Ahp-chagi*)

The flying front kick, also known as the jumping front kick, can be applied effectively to free fighting when you master it.

Those who cannot make a standing front kick can never make a flying front kick. Practicing the flying kick is a complete exercise which ultimately provides the best means of attaining balance, coordination, and body shifting.

Never kick a target placed higher than your eye level. Your upper body should remain erect, rather than be pressing forward too much. When kicking, avoid leaning backward to prevent falling. Furthermore, never let the kicking leg extend to its full length, because the thrusting power in delivering the kick can unbalance your whole body if the power is not controlled. In delivering the flying front kick, it is important to jump high enough into the air, because you might otherwise return to the floor before the completion of the kick, thereby losing your balance.

The flying front kick is a surprise attack, catching the opponent psychologically off-guard. The kick is executed in the air and the direction of the kick is not upward but in an advancing forward motion.

This kick is best applied by first forcing the opponent to retreat. Moving forward quickly with a flying motion adds to the power of your kick and also unbalances your opponent, rendering him less able to initiate an instant counterattack or a smothering block.

A flying front kick can be made in two ways: jumping on one foot and kicking with the other, or jumping and kicking with the same foot.

Jumping on One Foot and Kicking With the Other. Assuming back stance with your right leg forward, jump up and forward, simultaneously cocking your left leg for a flying kick. A short adjustment for distance by extending the front foot forward might help to add an advancing motion to the jump. As soon as your body reaches the highest point in the air, snap your left leg outward to the target and pull it back to the cocked position again and return to the floor. Note that, while in the air, your upper body is in a straight position twisting slightly to the left.

Jumping and Kicking With the Same Foot. Assuming back stance with your right leg forward, jump up with your right leg pushing your body forward after first bending and raising your left knee, so your whole weight is supported by your right leg. While jumping up with the right leg, cock it and snap out to the target. The kick is snapped out to the target and your upper body is simultaneously turned back to the right to retain balance. Then you return to the floor after pulling the kicking leg back into the cocked position. This type of flying front kick requires more body maneuvering, but provides a stronger kick, because, through the maneuver, the body directly backs up the kick; moreover, the distance from your opponent from which the kick can be delivered is greater than with the other type of flying front kick.

A double flying front kick can be applied by combining both types of flying front kicks; i.e., jumping with the right leg, making a fast snap kick with the left leg and then making another one with the right leg at the highest point in the air. This double kick should not be used frequently because both kicks are weak in power and timing. Furthermore you might easily get overcommitted and off-balance through the heavy body maneuvers required.

15 How to Use the Front Kick

THE MASTERY of the front kick gives a karate trainee many advantages over an opponent, and it is suggested that much of his time be devoted to perfecting it. The front kick is not only fast but also powerful, with the force transmitted directly from the body while maintaining a good balance. The combination of speed and balance allows the trainee many opportunities to use the front kick in conjunction with other techniques for a strong series of moves. The use of the front kick in free fighting does not require an overcommitment of the entire body, and combination attacks utilizing the front kick are hard to block.

There are several disadvantages in the application of the front kick. Since it must be executed from a front-facing posture, it usually leaves the trainee wide open to a counterattack. In addition, beginners often hurt their toes when executing front kicks in free fighting. Even though they are taught always to curl the toes upward, that is sometimes not enough to avoid injury. You should continually practice to make sure that your attacking foot travels in a straight line while aiming for the solar plexus. Also, you must make sure that the target at which you aim is open wide enough for the kick to reach it without the toes hitting first.

The front kick must be practiced over and over again, preferably carefully on a heavy bag till you master its safe application, so you can overcome the fear of hurting your own toes when using it in free fighting. Unless this fear is overcome, it usually prevents you from applying the front kick at opportune moments. In addition, it is always wise to prepare for a defense while delivering the front kick. You are advised to practice many sets of front kick combinations, so the sets can be applied in free fighting as well as a simple unit move.

● Basics for Front-Kick Application

Many free-fighting stances provide you with an excellent opportunity for the application of the front kick in free fighting. Forward stance, back stance, cat stance, and even stance can be utilized. Back stance is generally preferred as it gives the best posture; i.e., a half-facing posture. This posture can turn into a front-facing posture while delivering the kick with your rear foot, providing the most room for the foot to travel and therefore, the most power. Also, the distance between the two legs in back stance affords a comfortable balance both in defensive and offensive moves. When executing the kick from back stance, simply shift your weight from your rear leg to your forward leg, kicking at the same time. This transfer of the weight while moving forward adds to the power of the kick.

Placement of Arms While Delivering the Front Kick. You must hold your guarding arm in the right place while attacking with a front kick. When there is absolutely no danger of a counterattack while making a simple front-kick attack, you may place both your arms at your sides. In a series of attacking moves, your arms must be placed to guard at a ready position for the next attack against an opponent. The best position for the arm guard while delivering the kick is with one hand acting defensively and the other preparing for an offensive move. When prepared to act one or two moves ahead with the arm at the ready position, speed for combination attacks will be mustered easily.

Your left arm should stay in front of your body to be used for blocking in case of a counterattack or to deflect the opponent's guarding arm while kicking. Your right arm should be cocked to enable you to deliver a following punch if your kick does not reach the target. With such an arm placement, you should retain your balance strongly while making a front snap kick.

Twist your body forward, pushing your right arm forward into a defensive position, simultaneously executing the front thrust kick, which, if blocked, may be followed with a punch with your cocked left hand. If the kick and punch fail, you can always come down into a side-facing posture, able to defend safely with your front arm against counterattack.

Front Kick with the Front Foot (*Ahp-bal Ahp-chagi*). The front kick with the rear foot has already been explained in Section 14, but a front foot can be used to make a front kick in a stationary position when your opponent is close enough to you so that stepping or adjustment for distance is not required. This kick is usually delivered from cat stance in which there is almost no weight on your front foot, allowing an attack without much body maneuver. However, back stance or even stance are also suited for this kick, provided it is delivered correctly. This kick is applied as a fast attack in both initial and counterattacks even though it lacks the power of a killing technique.

Assuming back stance to make a front snap kick with the front foot, first raise your front leg and bring the lower part of your leg tightly toward the thigh with your knee up. Then snap it out to the target. Quickly bring the kicking foot back to the cocked position again, and lower it into the original back stance.

Opposite-Side-Facing Position. Trainees often do not attack with the correct foot, thereby making unnecessary motions or endangering themselves. The front kick must be executed by either the front or rear foot depending upon which of the kicker's feet is on the same side as his opponent's unprotected area. In general, for a strong front kick, the rear foot is preferred, because the distance between the two feet gives the kicker space in which to build power.

In an opposite-side-facing free-fighting position, a front kick is delivered with the front foot. The adjustment for distance is made by stepping forward with the rear foot first and then extending your front foot forward in a kick: a short adjustment for distance is made by bringing your rear foot close to the front foot, and a long one by placing it ahead of the front foot. Your movement of stepping forward while adjusting for distance imparts an advancing motion to your entire body, through which your kicking leg becomes cocked and swings out powerfully.

When the distance to adjust is not too great, as in most cases of free fighting, you can shorten the distance by bringing your rear foot close to your front foot and then making the kick. In a short adjustment for distance, the kick is often delivered in a hopping motion which speeds up delivery. In this move your body position does not have to be changed at all. The movement should be made as smoothly as possible so the whole move is performed as in a simple unit kick.

When an adjustment for a long distance is needed, merely place the rear foot as far ahead of the front foot as necessary, maintaining balance and shifting weight. You will be open to an instant counterattack unless you are particularly careful not to twist your body too far forward while adjusting for a long distance.

Same Side-Facing Position. If necessary, adjust for distance by extending your front foot forward. This fast movement often escapes your opponent's notice and scores on him whether he is defending by arm blocking or shifting backward. The front kick with the rear foot and the adjustment for distance must be executed as if they were a single unit move. The momentum created by the extension of the front foot assists body advancement and adds power to your kick.

Front Kick from an Oblique Direction. An opponent who maintains a tight guard covering his front-facing area but leaves an opening on the front of his body can best be reached by a roundhouse kick, a hook punch, or a palm-heel strike following an adjustment for distance. However, a front kick can also be effectively applied from an oblique direction where the attacker faces an opening directly. Actually, in this situation, the one who attacks with a front kick is much safer from counterattack than one who uses hand attacks, and the front kick is speedier than other kicks since it requires less body maneuver.

While adjusting for distance, extend your front foot forward, not straight toward the opponent but slightly inward at an oblique angle to the direction of his forward motion. Pivot your front foot while cocking the rear leg and simultaneously thrust the front kick all in one continuous motion. The cocking motion of your rear leg toward the opponent helps pivot the supporting foot and your body twists accordingly.

This type of move is particularly good when your opponent stands in a side-facing posture and does not guard his front body. The adjustment for distance in an inward oblique angle must be performed quickly and smoothly, and the twisting and kicking must be executed as if the whole move is one single unit.

Spot-Pushing Front Kick (*Meelmyu Ahp-chagi*). The spot-pushing front kick can be made by either the front or rear foot. When the kick is delivered with the rear foot, the distance is shortened by pushing the whole body slightly forward toward the opponent with the front foot. When the kick is executed with the front foot, the body is pushed forward by the rear foot while the front leg rises to the cocked position and snaps out toward the opponent. This type of kick is very weak, but can be effective as a speedy snap kick. It can be applied against the opponent who moves around quickly with short spot shifting (see Section 8 on Spot Shifting). Sometimes even when a fast adjustment for distance for a strong front kick is detected by the opponent, the spot-pushing kick can be used as a substitute for the strong front kick originally intended to be used.

Shift the body weight to your front foot while raising your rear leg to the cocked position as if you were making a front thrust kick without an adjustment for distance. While it is being cocked, simultaneously push your body toward the opponent with the front foot. While returning the front foot (left) to the floor, deliver the kick with the right foot in a snapping motion of the kicking knee. The pushing forward move should begin as soon as the kicking leg reaches the line of the supporting leg. Consequently the whole move is performed as if it were a simple front kick. You may initiate the move with a fake punch to ensure that there is no danger for your initial attack. Hand attacks may be effectively combined with the spot-pushing front kick.

This kick is somewhat different from the flying front kick which reaches further but requires greater body maneuvers. The spot-pushing front kick is weaker in power but its smaller and speedier movements often escape detection.

● Front Kick in Combination Attack

Many different attacks may be effectively combined with an initial front snap or thrust kick. The kick puts the defending opponent off balance or forces him into a defensive position, enabling the kicker to pursue the situation to his advantage.

Front Kick and Hand Attacks. An initial kick executed with power and balance often leaves you in a good position to continue attacking with various hand techniques such as the fist punch, the elbow punch, the knuckle punch, and the palm-heel strike.

When your kick is arm blocked, continue with a fist punch as soon as the kicking foot returns to the floor. The kick and punch should be delivered almost simultaneously. Even if the opponent defends against the kick by shifting backward, you can continue with the punch by stepping forward following the return of the kicking leg to the floor, thus shortening the distance and extending the attack.

Simultaneous Combination Attacks. When both free fighters are closely guarded, the simultaneous execution of a front kick and punch will often score. This combination is best applied when the opponent defends without shifting away. However, both the kick and punch in a simultaneous combination attack are usually weak in power.

When you are in a tightly guarded position and the opponent is about to attack, you can control the distance and counter by attacking him first. A simultaneous execution of a front kick and fist punch may surprise him and score. First, raise your right knee for the kick while cocking your right fist. Execute the kick and punch simultaneously, the punch pushing out mostly with arm power, and the kick lacking the force of the advancing body. To finish the opponent with a strong attack, follow immediately with a reverse punch with your left fist. A forward fist punch is also possible, by bringing your arm back to the cocked position after returning your kicking foot to the floor, following the simultaneous combination attack.

Front Snap Kick and Following Kicks. A fast thrust kick with the rear foot following the snap kick often scores against an opponent who habitually defends against a front kick by shifting away. A flying front kick can also be applied following the snap kick.

If the opponent shifts away from an initial kick attack, the kicking foot should be returned quickly to the floor. Then adjust for distance by stepping forward with your rear foot and execute another front kick with your kicking foot. (If there had been an opening on the opponent's front-facing ribs, the kick would have been made with your left foot without adjusting for distance.)

In order to save the time and motion of the adjustment for distance, a subsequent attack can be made by employing a flying front kick. Be careful to guard against an instant counterattack while making the flying kick.

If the opponent shifts far away from your initial attack, bring your kicking foot to the floor in a forward motion to follow him. Jump up with the same leg pushing your entire body straight forward toward your retreating opponent, and simultaneously deliver the flying front kick and return to a balanced position.

If your opponent shifts back moving his front area to the other side, just kick with your other foot after you have jumped up in the air. You can, however, take as many steps as you need to adjust for the right distance before jumping.

● Front-Thrust Kick Following Faking Moves

Since you must expose your front torso while delivering a front kick, your opponent can arm block the kick without moving back in order to make a fast counterattack. You can, by using a faking move, break the block and the threatened counterattack, and create an opening for a front-thrust kick. In general, the fake is made with either hand in a punching or striking motion and also by a sudden strike or grab at your opponent's guarding arm.

Faking With the Rear Hand to Kick With the Rear Foot. While faking with the rear hand, the body becomes momentarily twisted into a front-facing posture where the rear foot faces the target in a straight direction. The hand also serves as a guard when the kick is delivered.

Make a short punch in a pushing or snapping motion toward the opponent's high target to fake him into raising his guarding arm while pulling your rear foot into the cocked position for a front kick, keeping your own targets guarded with your front arm. Since the punch is a fake, it does not require full strength. The front kick must be delivered immediately following the fake.

Deflecting the Guarding Arm While Adjusting for Distance. Your opponent may sometimes be disconcerted when his front-guarding arm is deflected by your fist. You can score with a front kick during this moment of shock. An adjustment for distance must accompany your deflecting move.

First deflect your opponent's guarding arm with your front arm in a sharp and snappy motion to open him up, simultaneously adjusting for distance in a hopping motion concluded with a front kick. Your front arm must still function as a guard in case of an instant counter-attack.

● Front-Fake Kick to Adjust for Distance

The fake is executed by making the motions of a front kick without actually kicking. Raise your knee as if you are about to kick, but, instead of delivering the kick, just push it forward and step down to close the distance between you and your opponent. This type of action often causes your opponent to move, leaving himself open to an immediate subsequent attack. It not only confuses your opponent, but the raised knee acts as an additional guard for your middle and low target areas.

Front-Fake Kick for Knife-Hand Strike. When your opponent responds to your initial attack, you can sometimes fool him by employing your rear foot in a front-kick motion. The kicking leg must come straight down or slightly forward depending on the distance you need for your following move. (Or you can return to your original stance if needed.) Proceed then with a strike, punch, or kick.

Front-Fake Kick For the Front-Thrust Kick. The front kick used as a fake is a snappy but pushing forward move, executed from a well-guarded position. When you reach the proper distance, execute a front-thrust kick with your other foot (the right foot in the picture).

In this case, a flying front kick may also be applied by jumping up with either foot and kicking with the right foot. When your opponent defends with an arm block but with little shifting, as above, you can jump up and kick with the right foot before your left foot returns to the floor. Sometimes, a fake with the front hand prior to the fake kick forces your opponent to shift thereby eliminating the possibility of an instant counterattack by him while you are jumping. If your fake causes him to shift far back, catch up with him by leaping forward in the air on the kicking leg after returning it to the floor in forward stance.

Flying Fake for a Hand Attack (*Dtuymyu Chigi*). Sometimes, a flying motion is used only to shorten the distance between you and your opponent so your punch or strike may score while the defending opponent is not expecting it. While in the air, your kicking leg should be cocked to protect your low and middle target areas and to provide better coordination against the opponent's instant counterattack than if both of your legs were down.

Transfer your body weight to your front foot while lifting your rear foot from the ground. Jump up toward your opponent with the front foot high in the air, simultaneously cocking the rear leg in front of your body. Then punch his face when the right distance is attained, being sure to guard against his counterattack while returning to the floor.

16 Defense Against the Front Kick

To DEFEND against the front-kick attack, in addition to being accurate with your arm blocks, you must be relaxed, using your arms in their guarding position to cover most of your front-facing area. Your posture should be well set. A side-facing posture frequently affords your opponent less of an opening. A half-front-facing posture, while less desirable for defensive purposes, usually permits easy shifting into a position for counterattacks. The best defense is one that combines defensive moves with offensive moves which may prevent your opponent from following through with successive combination attacks.

When you become familiar with all the techniques of the front-kick attack, you may plan your defense accordingly. With good reflexes, speed, coordination, and balance, you should be able to apply the best combinations of defense and offense interchangeably, thereby enabling you to exploit the free-fighting situation to your advantage.

● Simple Defense

Many defensive moves are applied against the various methods of front-kick attacks. It is always important to master the simple blocks from many different positions.

Arm Block. The arm block is the most important defense against a front-kick attack. The most frequently used arm block against a front kick attack is the low block—downward, outward, or inward, appropriate for the way your opponent's attack is executed. Some prefer the downward block at all times while others use only the outward block. However, you should try to master all forms of the block for use in combined moves.

The low block, both downward and outward, has already been explained in Section 9. The inward low block is performed with either surface of the forearms, which strike in an inward direction from the outside of the body line. Even if the block is delivered speedily, it is a weak one, and consequently best used in combination with body shifting.

While blocking, pull your front arm toward the front part of your body, bending the elbow and utilizing the arm power only in a small motion.

An X-block is sometimes applied against a strong front kick attack. A double arm block is used to provide a double guard for vital targets. The use of these blocks is identical to the single arm block and they are seldom used in free fighting except when you are put at a disadvantage from unexpected attacks.

Shifting. Shifting is an excellent defense against a front-kick attack, because the combination attack, which plays an important role in the front-kick application, cannot easily be utilized by the attacker when the defender controls the distance by body shifting. Shifting moves combined with arm blocks are the best defense against combination attacks. Usually, arm blocks are combined with a shift when the distance covered is short, since the attacker can easily continue his combination attacks with a fast adjustment for distance.

The opponent's front-thrust kick could have scored if the defender's short shift was not combined with his arm block. It is also possible that, if the kick was not blocked strongly, the attacker would have continued with a combination attack, since he had already adjusted for distance and was close enough for the convenient application of hand attacks.

When the front kick is delivered at close range, a spot shift works effectively. Placing your front arm to cover the front-facing area, you can shift and change into a side-facing posture so that less of an opening faces your opponent directly. Consequently, defense against the front-kick attack with a combination of shifting, arm blocking, and keeping the body posture in a sideway position is safer than any single unit defensive move.

Smothering Block (*Putitchyu Makgi*). The smothering block against the front-kick attack is seldom used in free fighting. However, it can be applied in combination with a counter punch against a front-fake kick designed to create openings for other kicks. The smothering block is performed by advancing toward your opponent in a side-facing posture and raising your front knees to protect your vital targets, simultaneously deflecting his kicking leg with the flat of your front foot as the opponent initiates a front-kick move. This type of block only works when you correctly predict the attacker's initial move.

Push your body slightly forward with your right knee up and your left hand cocked, the right arm in a guarding position to deflect your opponent's initial front kick with the flat of your front foot. Any punch combined with his kick should be blocked by your guarding right arm while looking for an opening for a counterattack with your left hand which has already been cocked.

● Counterattack Against the Simple Front Kick

The downward, outward, and inward low blocks are always interchangeable with each other, and many punches and strikes are applicable for a counterattack following low blocks.

Reverse Fist Punch. Assuming that your left leg is forward in a same-side-facing position, make an outward low block with your front arm against your opponent's front-kick attack. The block is preferably combined with a short backward shift far enough back to knock his kicking leg outward so that an opening is created. Then follow with a reverse middle punch against his kidney or left rib cage under his arm. Your left arm should guard against your opponent's potential following attack until the counter punch is completed.

Front Kick. When your opponent combines a front kick with his hand attacks, you are much safer in counterattacking with a kick rather than with hand attacks. Your arms must always be employed to guard. After making a downward block first against your opponent's kick, simultaneously deliver a front kick with your front foot, unless the distance between you and your opponent is great enough to permit you to make a rear leg kick, which is much stronger.

Circle-Stepping Block and Fist Punch (*Tolmyu Makgo-chigi*). The circle-stepping block is an inward arm block executed while stepping in a circle to your back with your rear foot. A back-fist punch with your blocking arm and or reverse punch are recommended for counterattack. Since the block often results in a shortened distance between you and your opponent, he may be able to combine with hand attacks before your counter punch is delivered. Therefore, this type of block is sometimes performed while you are shifting the entire body backward, thereby maintaining a safer distance.

Assuming that your opponent makes a front-thrust kick in a same-side-facing position, shift your rear leg backward in a circling motion causing your front foot to pivot, simultaneously making an inward low block with your front arm. Continue the blocking motion with your front arm to cock it in front of your body preparatory to a back-fist punch and snap it out toward the opponent's solar plexus. Instead, you might use the front arm to guard your front-facing area, if needed. You can also execute a reverse fist punch as an additional counterattack.

● Counter Shifting (*Pahng-kong Yeedong*)

Counter shifting means defending with an initial body shift and then employing a counter-attack accompanied by a shift toward your opponent with an appropriate adjustment for distance. This method of defense is often important in defending against front-kick attack combination moves. The shift helps to provide a safer defense and the immediate creation of an opening for a counterattack.

Straight Back and Forth. Against a front-kick attack you can defend by simple stepping backward either with single or multiple shifts, or with a straight backward move. This can be followed immediately by a shift back toward your opponent with counter moves either by simple stepping forward or by a straight forward move.

When your opponent thrusts a front kick with his rear foot from his same-side-facing position, you can defend with a simple stepping backward shift with full speed. (Or you can shift straight backward instead.) You can combine a short arm block with your shift to make your defense safer. The first shift should put you in a well-balanced, downward position so that your whole body becomes poised and agile. Then counterattack immediately with a front-thrust kick (or a punch, side kick, roundhouse kick, etc.) while shifting your body toward the opponent following an appropriate adjustment for distance.

Ninety-Degree Open Shift and Counterattack. Angle shifting often creates openings on the opponent for a counterattack. When you defend by shifting ninety degrees to the side, your opponent is not easily able to adjust to the new position since the momentum of his front-thrust kick carries him straight forward. The direction of your shift depends on your opponent's attack as well as the defensive position needed for a counter move. Some prefer a wide angle shift while others prefer a narrower one. In any case, the shifting distance must be considerable to avoid your opponent's possible combination attacks and the direction of the shift is such that you might spot an open target area for your counterattack.

When your opponent attacks with a front-thrust kick, shift away to a new position at some distance from him so that your front leg becomes your rear leg and your rear leg your front leg. In the shift your rear leg almost immediately follows your front leg to which your body weight should be transferred. Your body posture should preferably be side facing your opponent. Then counterattack with a front-thrust kick while your attacker is attempting to compensate for the direction of your counter move. (A counterattack is also possible with a side punch, side kick, right hand punch, etc.) This type of shift is a surprise move, but be careful to retain your balance and guard.

Part VII Side-Kick Moves
(Yup Chagi)

17 How to Make the Side Kick

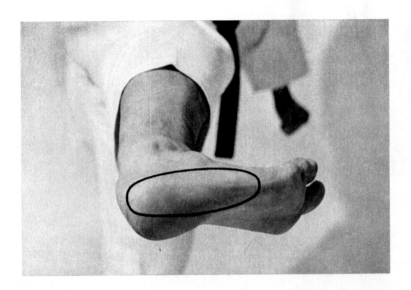

MANY KARATE (*tae-kwon do*) trainees have found that the side kick is very difficult to execute. In making the side kick, many unaccustomed body moves must be performed. Many trainees find it hard to open the leg to the side and stretch the muscles and simultaneously maintain their balance while delivering a side kick. The side kick requires total coordination because it involves the use of the whole body. The side edge of the foot is used as a striking surface with the part closer to the heel for harder targets. The ankle of the kicking foot must be flexed toward the inside of the leg with the big toe pointing slightly downward.

With the side kick you can attack most of the body's vital points. The main targets for the side kick are the ribs, solar plexus, and face. The side kick has distinct advantages over other types of kicks when it is applied effectively in free fighting. It can reach a considerably longer distance, so the kicker is not in immediate danger of instant counterattack from his opponent while delivering the kick in free fighting. Furthermore, execution of the kick in side stance in a side-facing posture leaves the kicker less open to counterattack.

The disadvantages of the side kick are that it usually leaves the kicker in an awkward position for continuing his attack. The leg can be easily grabbed and the kicker can be pulled off balance. Consequently, delivering a powerful side kick is not easy to do and requires much diligent practice. However, if you master the side kick you will be able to execute it in a completely natural motion.

There are many types of side kicks: the side limbering-up kick, side-rising kick, side thrust kick, side snap kick, and flying side kick.

● Side Limbering-Up Kick (*Yup Ohlligi*)

As with the limbering-up front kick, the primary purpose of the side limbering-up kick is to stretch the muscles under the legs and loosen the joints used in other side kicks, so that kicks such as the side-rising kick and side thrust kick can be performed smoothly and effectively without strain. A very powerful side kick can damage the kicker's own joints or muscles, unless his body is completely loosened up beforehand. For this reason it is important to include the side limbering-up kick in your daily exercises.

To make a side limbering-up kick with your right leg, assume side stance. Cross your left foot over the right (the left foot can also be placed alongside or behind the right) and then raise your right leg to the side and toward the body with the knee straight. As the leg is lifted, the upper body should lean toward the right side, with the supporting knee slightly bent, and the supporting foot flat on the ground. Flex the ankle of the kicking foot toward the inside of the leg, pressing the outer edge of the foot away from you. Maintain this position until you complete the side limbering-up kick. Bring the kicking foot from the air back to the body line and return to another side stance position. Never lean your upper body backward to achieve height, for this will result in a complete loss of balance.

● Side-Rising Kick (*Yup Cha-ohlligi*)

The side-rising kick is delivered in a rising direction with a snapping motion of the knee. A fast delivery of the rising kick acts as an uppercut with shocking impact. It is best applied against a target that leans toward the kick in a steady position. While delivering the kick, the body must be in a well-balanced position, which usually permits easy follow through with a good combination attack. The main targets are solar plexus, chin, etc.

Assuming side stance for a side kick with the left foot, cock your left leg, bending the knee and drawing it back to the supporting knee. (Or, you can take one step with your right foot to your left side first and then prepare to kick.) Raise your left foot in an arc while snapping it out from the knee. Do not execute this kick in the same way as a side limbering-up kick by bringing it straight up, but direct it up and outward toward your target. Immediately after kicking, bring the leg back to the cocked position and then return promptly to the side stance. While kicking, your upper body remains upright, leaning slightly in the direction of the kick.

The side-rising kick is a form of side snap kick which utilizes the snapping motion of the kicking knee, with full striking force at the point of impact, as in the front snap kick or snap punch. The side snap kick, which is applied to any type of side kick, can be delivered to the high, middle, and low target areas with good balance retained. However, you must be particularly careful not to extend the kicking leg its full distance when it is delivered in a sideway direction traveling parallel to the floor, because the snapping motion might pull the joints of the kicking knee or leg unless the force is controlled so the leg is pulled back at the last minute before it is fully extended. Injuries might occur among beginners who have not mastered the timing and do not stop the snapping motion and bring the kicking leg back to the body.

● Side Thrust Kick (*Yup Cha-tzirugi*)

Many trainees frequently use the side thrust kick in free fighting. It can be a killing attack if it is delivered with full power. It provides trainees with a means of reaching a distant target from a well-guarded position. The side thrust kick can be and is often grabbed by the opponent unless delivered swiftly with full power or followed by a second agile action with or after the kick.

To make a side thrust kick with the left foot, assume side stance and step with your right foot over (or behind) the left and then bend your left knee, bringing the left leg up on your left side with the foot close to the supporting knee. Then raise the kicking foot attempting to face it directly to the target and simultaneously extend it straight out to the side almost parallel to the floor with the full power of your hip and upper body. The mere act of pushing your leg out is not enough for a killing blow. You must thrust your hip strongly into the kick to provide additional power transmission from the body to the foot. After the kick, pull your kicking leg back to the cocked position and return to side stance. Note that when executing the kick, the toes of the supporting foot pivot outward at a slight angle.

● Rising-Heel Kick (*Yup Duiro-chagi*)

Some confuse this kick with the side thrust kick, but there are differences in execution, power, and effect. Both have advantages as well as disadvantages. The rising-heel kick is delivered with the hip of the kicking leg facing the target, and the direction of power is more toward the back than toward the side. The side thrust kick travels parallel to the floor, the side-rising kick arcs up into the target, but the rising-heel kick travels in a straight, upward angle to the target.

To make a rising-heel kick in side stance, cock the left leg slightly in front of the right knee. The left heel and hip should face the target. Thrust out your heel directly toward the target maintaining the hip in the same position. Return the left leg to side stance after first pulling it back to the cocked position.

● Flying Side Kick (*Dtuiyu Yup-chagi*)

The flying side kick, or, as some call it, the jumping side kick, is an advanced technique when applied in free fighting. As with the flying front kick, it can be executed in two ways: jumping on one foot and kicking with the other foot, or jumping and kicking with the same foot.

Some people attempt to distinguish between them by describing a flying side kick as one in which the kicker travels straight up in the air and then delivers the kick, and a jumping side kick as one in which he travels directly toward the target simultaneously delivering the kick. However, both types of the execution of the kick will be called a flying side kick. The normal target for this kick is almost any vital spot such as the solar plexus, face, neck, chin, ribs, and even the knees. A thrusting motion is used more often than a snapping one.

In delivering a flying side kick more emphasis must be placed on balance than in delivering a flying front kick, as the former is more easily blocked. While in the air, the upper body should be twisted in the kicking direction. Never execute a flying side kick that requires you to kick higher than your own chest. The flying side kick can be used advantageously; its main qualities being the shortening of distance between you and your opponent, its surprise value, and the fact that it enables you to catch up with an opponent while maintaining a side-facing posture thus avoiding exposing your own middle target area.

The flying side kick should not be applied often in free fighting because you may lose your balance completely when your kick is defended by a strong arm block. Do not attempt to reach out for an opponent while in the air; if the distance changes and you are too close or too far for a perfect kick, withdraw the kicking leg and return to a balanced position as quickly as possible. Never lean back, so that even when strongly blocked, your balance is less subject to being upset.

Jumping With One Foot and Kicking With the Other. Assume back stance to make a flying side kick with the left foot. Jump up with your right foot, cocking both legs. Your body must leap as a compact unit and not in various individual parts in order to get the best coordination and power. Then, extend your left leg in a straight line toward the target. The upper body maintains its posture and is twisted slightly in the direction of the kick. Cock your kicking leg back to the body line and return to the ground in back stance. Note that the target is continually kept on your side until the kick is completed.

Jumping and Kicking With the Same Foot. To make a flying side kick with your right foot, assume back stance with the right leg forward. (You can also start with side stance or other stances to make the flying kick.) Jump on the right foot, cocking both legs. Then extend your right foot straight out to the side toward the target. After kicking, return the kicking leg back to the cocked position and come back to the floor in back stance.

18 How to Use the Side Kick

MANY TRAINEES use the side kick more than any other in free fighting because there is less chance of injury to the toes than with the front or roundhouse kick. Also, the side-facing posture gives less opening to the opponent than a front-facing posture.

Unless the side kick is skillfully applied in free fighting, it often leads to an overcommitment of the body. The unnatural body movements required usually hamper a trainee's speed and balance. It is important to make sure the kicking leg is neither grabbed nor blocked too hard by the opponent in order to maintain good balance.

The side thrust kick is good as a strong, single attack, but the side snap and side-rising kicks are preferable in conjunction with a series of other attacks. In general, the side kick can also be used as an instant counterattack, not so much for the purpose of scoring a point, but to disrupt the opponent's initial attack and to unbalance him. Practice the side kick on both stationary and slowly moving bags.

● Basics of Side-Kick Application

The side kick should be practiced from many different free-fighting stances. Whatever stance the kick originates from, the body always turns so the target is directly on the side. The turning of the body, the motion of cocking the leg and extending it toward the target all must always be performed at full speed as if they were a simple unit move.

As with any other kick, the side kick can be delivered either with the front foot or with the rear foot. However, the rear foot is seldom used for an initial kick due to the extreme amount of body maneuver needed to bring it into play. When executing a side kick with the rear foot in free fighting, the necessary body rotation may take a lot of unnecessary time, resulting in a slow motion and danger from opening your own front-facing area to the opponent's instant counterattack.

In making a side kick with the rear foot, an adjustment for distance is frequently made simply by extending the front foot forward prior to bringing the rear foot to the cocked position.

Assuming the opponent's rib cage is the main target, it does not make much difference which of your feet completes the kick as long as it is delivered straight into the target from your side. The side kick with the front foot is a favorite of free fighters. However, such a move takes training as it requires one or more adjustments for distance to get in correct range of the target. The whole move must be accomplished with speed and agility for its successful execution.

Placement of Arms While Delivering the Side Kick. Placement of the arms depends on the moves to follow the execution of the kick. Some prefer to place the forward arm across the front of the body, and others extend it out to the rear. Placement across the front of the body allows you to make a higher kick as it opens the muscles on the side and keeps them from interfering with the kick. Also, when your kicking leg is caught or blocked hard, you may continue with a back-fist punch to save your position. The rear arm is usually placed in a guarding or cocked position while delivering the kick.

However, such placement of the arm is not highly advised as it tends to weaken your position because it hinders the upper body from moving into the target with balance and power. If your kicking leg is caught by the opponent, for example, it might have been better to have placed your forward arm behind the kicking leg because it would have allowed you room to rotate your body to face the opponent directly while pulling your leg back to the cocked position. (For further study, see Section 20 on "When the Kicking Leg Is Grabbed.")

Side Kick With the Front Foot. When an adjustment for distance is not required, the side kick with the front foot in a stationary position must be performed almost like the front kick with the front foot; i.e., raising the kicking leg to cock it first and then kicking.

To make a side kick with the front foot, assume a cat stance free-fighting position. First, cock the front leg while at the same time turning your front-facing side to the opponent. Snap out the kick and bring it back in one motion to the cocked position, and then return to cat stance. The kick is executed while the body remains static.

Adjustment for Distance by Stepping Forward. To execute a side kick with the front foot from a proper free-fighting distance, an adjustment for distance can be made by stepping forward first with the rear foot.

Assume back stance as a free-fighting position. To execute a side kick with the front (left) foot, first adjust for distance by stepping forward with your right leg, placing it ahead of your front foot with its toes facing to the right and simultaneously thrusting your body toward the right, so the target is on your left side. Make sure the kick is delivered straight toward the target after the leg is cocked. Otherwise, the kick will move in an arc from the rear to the front, wasting power and ruining accuracy.

The side kick with the front foot can be made in two steps. First, extend your front foot forward from a back stance free-fighting position and simultaneously follow it with the rear foot. Then, the kick is executed while your entire body weight rests on the rear foot. These two moves must be well coordinated with the kick and all made as if they were one simple adjustment. Even a long distance can be short-ened through this type of combined adjustment for distance.

Adjustment for Distance by Short Stepping. To make a side kick with the front foot while free fighting at a fairly close range, a short adjustment for distance can be made by simply bringing the rear foot close to the front foot. You must practice this type of stepping constantly to be fast enough to kick as soon as the rear foot touches the floor, so that the whole move appears to be made in a single hopping motion.

To make a side thrust kick with the front (left) foot in a back stance position, bring your rear foot forward toward the front foot. As it is placed on the floor having completed the adjustment for distance, execute the kick simultaneously, in a simple motion of first cocking and thrusting out to the target.

To obtain maximum speed, you may adjust for distance in a hopping motion; i.e., cocking your front leg while advancing the rear and extending the front leg toward the target as the rear touches the floor. If the distance for the kick is still too great when the rear touches the floor, you may execute a spot-pushing side kick which will be explained later in this section.

Adjustment for Distance by Stepping Behind. A side kick with the front foot, especially a rising-heel kick, can often be executed by using another type of adjustment for distance which is performed by stepping behind the front foot with the rear foot. While making this move, your body twists, thereby exposing your kidney to the instant counterattack of your opponent. You must guard the kidney by placing your front-guarding arm backward or by using a fake move to offset a counterattack.

To step forward with the rear (right) foot behind the front foot in order to adjust for distance, twist your body slightly backward so the side part of your left shoulder faces the opponent, pivoting your left heel forward. Simultaneously step forward with the rear foot passing behind your front (left) foot and make a rising-heel kick with the front foot after cocking it.

If your back becomes too exposed to the opponent, it means that you twisted your body too much, or that the opponent anticipated your move and moved slightly to the side while you were stepping. In this case, you can deliver the kick in an arc with a hooking motion; i.e., a hook kick which will be explained in Part IX.

A long distance can also be shortened by the combination of double stepping. Make a short adjustment by extending the front foot slightly forward first and then adding another adjustment by stepping behind the front foot with the other foot.

Spot-Pushing Side Kick (*Meelmyu Yup-chagi***).** The spot-pushing side kick is often delivered with the front foot in order to execute the whole move smoothly without an adjustment for distance. It is a side kick which is executed with the front foot, by pushing the whole body forward with the rear foot while cocking the kicking leg. It is a short and speedy kick aimed at the front-facing ribs or lower area, but it lacks power, because it is mostly delivered in a pushing move in conjunction with a snapping motion. This type of kick often scores at a fairly close distance, since the opponent, not detecting your steps for adjustment for distance, does not expect your kick to reach him.

To make a spot-pushing side kick with the front (left) foot from a side-facing posture in a back stance position, raise your front foot, simultaneously pushing your body forward with your rear foot in a hopping motion. Pushing is made with a jerking motion of body advancement and must cover only a short distance. As the rear foot is placed on the floor following the pushing, extend your front foot to the target with the advancing force of the body.

● Side Kick in Combination Attacks

Body maneuver associated with delivering side kicks may result in weak and slow moves for side-kick combination attacks. However, there are some moves that can be suitably combined with a side kick in free fighting.

Side Snap Kick and Hand Attacks. In order to combine some hand attacks in conjunction with an initial side-kick move, a side snap kick is preferable to a thrust kick. A side or back-fist punch, or a knife-hand strike, which are made by the hand on the same side as the kicking leg, can often follow as secondary attacks. A reverse fist punch or palm-heel strike can also be used in a twisting motion of the body following the kick.

In an opposite-side-facing position, your initial side snap kick to the opponent's ribs can cause him to make an unnecessary downward block. You can cock the kicking leg quickly back to your body line while cocking the same-side fist. Then, thrust a side-fist punch as the leg returns to side stance. If the kick is arm blocked in a more outward direction, a back-fist blow with the hand will score effectively. If the block is made in an inward direction, a reverse fist punch or a palm-heel strike will score. Even if your side kick is aimed at his ribs and deflected by the block, you can proceed with the side-fist punch.

Simultaneous Combination Attacks. A side-rising kick and a short back-fist punch can be combined for simultaneous execution in free fighting. However, the kick and punch executed simultaneously result in a weak move when compared with either the kick or punch executed as a single move. Despite its lack of full power, this type of combination attack is good for putting an opponent off guard when he defends by just using arm blocks without body shifting.

To perform a side-rising kick and a hand attack simultaneously, cock both foot and fist of the front side after first adjusting for distance. Execute both attacks simultaneously. While the opponent is caught off guard from the unexpected execution of the kick and a bottom-fist attack, you can return the kicking leg into forward stance and follow through with a reverse middle punch (or palm-heel strike).

Side-Rising Kick and Other Kicks. Both a side-rising kick and snap kick are often used to check the opponent if he defends by shifting backward. When a rising-heel kick is quickly followed by a side-rising kick in free fighting, fast adjustment for distance between the two kicks is important. You must catch your opponent with the rising-heel kick while he has not recovered from defending against the first kick.

After making a side-rising kick from a well-balanced position, return the kicking leg to the floor in a side-facing posture. Then, thrust out the rising-heel kick with the same foot after adjusting for distance by bringing the rear foot behind the front foot.

A flying side kick can also be combined with the side-rising kick effectively, since the flying motion instantly shortens the distance. To execute the flying kick immediately after the rising kick, return your kicking leg to the floor in side stance with a rapid momentary shifting of the body weight to that leg. This shift of weight should enable you to instantly jump up with the same leg, advancing straight toward the opponent and kicking with the same leg while in the air.

After returning your kicking leg (left) to the floor in a side-facing posture following the initial rising-kick attack, jump up toward him with your left foot and execute a flying side kick with the same.

If the distance is still great after the initial side-rising kick, an extra step can be made to adjust for distance, followed by a flying side kick which is made after jumping up with one leg and kicking with the other foot.

● Side-Thrust Kick Following a Faking Move

When your opponent is guarding his front-facing area tightly, it is difficult to score with a simple side kick. To loosen the tight guard and create openings for a successful side kick, some faking moves often precede the kick.

Fake With the Front Arm to Kick With the Same Side Foot. Raising a hand toward the opponent's face sometimes makes him block instinctively to protect his face, leaving his middle area open for a side-kick attack. Faking with the front fist and correctly adjusting for distance to make the kick with the front foot must be done simultaneously.

In a same-side-facing position, start your faking move by pushing out your front fist to attract the opponent's attention to it, simultaneously adjusting for distance. Without hesitation, thrust your side kick with the front foot out to his ribs or chest. While faking with the fist, be careful of the opponent's instant counterattack. Instead, you can mislead him by deflecting his front-guarding arm with your front arm.

A flying side kick can be followed by a fake punch in order to save steps for an adjustment for distance.

Assuming a same-side-facing position as above, push your front fist toward the opponent and, at the same time, extend your front foot slightly forward. While he is defending against the fist move, make a short jump and kick with your front foot. The whole move must be performed with full speed as if a single unit.

Thrusting the Rear Arm Forward to Kick With the Rear Foot. This side thrust kick with the rear foot is delivered following a fake punch with the same-side fist. This type of move works particularly well against an opponent who habitually defends with arm blocks without much body shifting.

In a same-side-facing position, first thrust your rear fist forward toward the opponent's high target area. This thrusting arm motion helps not only to mislead your opponent but also to thrust your body weight forward, simultaneously relieving your rear foot of its supporting function. In a side-facing posture, cock the rear foot for a side kick and then thrust it out to the opponent's midsection area.

● Side Fake Kick to Adjust for Distance

The motion of cocking a side-kicking leg or lifting it forward is generally considered a side fake kick. Since this fake is simply a camouflage for adjusting for distance, most of the faking moves in this section can be replaced by a single successful adjustment for distance. However, the fake is often used because it is performed in a side-facing posture, against which the opponent has less opening for a counterattack. Additionally, while advancing, your lifted knee often covers your middle and low target areas against possible instant counterattacks.

Fake for a Knife-Hand Strike in a Hopping Motion. This move works effectively while the opponent is defending against your side kick with an arm block. After a side fake kick, an outward knife-hand strike, back-fist punch, side punch, or reverse palm-heel strike can be executed with a hopping motion of an adjustment for distance.

To attack with a knife-hand strike following a fake motion with the front foot in a same-side-facing position, bring the rear foot to the front in an adjustment for distance and simultaneously push your body forward with it while raising the front knee as if you were going to make a side kick with the front foot. Then jump up toward your opponent who is expecting your side kick, and execute an outward knife-hand strike while your body is returning to the floor in a side-facing posture. The entire body should be advanced forward in a single motion, preferably a hopping motion, the arm being cocked for a hand attack. The knife-hand strike also can be executed simultaneously with the supporting foot's return to the floor.

Fake for a Front-Thrust Kick. This fake is employed to make the opponent move so he can be caught with a fast-following kick while he is shifting. Stepping in with the faking move enables you to shorten the distance for a rear foot kick, without your opponent detecting your adjustment for distance.

Assuming a same-side-facing position, first fake your opponent with a side-kick motion with your front foot, pushing your body weight slightly forward following with an adjustment for distance. As your opponent steps backward, follow him by stepping down with the kicking leg into forward stance and simultaneously execute a front-thrust kick with the rear foot. (You can execute a roundhouse kick, instead.)

Fake for a Flying Side Kick. If the distance between you and your opponent is too great to execute a conventional, simple roundhouse or front kick because your opponent has shifted too far back, you could score with a flying side kick or a flying front kick.

There are several ways of executing a flying side kick following a faking move. After threatening your opponent with a side fake kick with your left foot in an opposite-side-facing free-fighting position, you can adjust for distance by stepping forward with your left foot into side stance and jump and kick with the same foot. Or, as soon as the left foot comes down into side stance, step forward with the right foot and jump with it, kicking with the left. A third way is to step down with your left foot into forward stance, simultaneously rotating your body to the left. Then jump sideway on your left foot and kick with the right foot, or first step forward with the right foot in a side-facing position and then jump and kick with the right foot.

After returning the fake leg (left) into forward stance, rotate your body slightly to the left to put the opponent on your right side. Simultaneously jump up toward the opponent on your left foot and snap out the right foot from the air at the last moment.

Rising-Heel Kick From an Oblique Direction. When the opponent stands in a side-facing posture with a tight guard and his front-facing area well protected, a simple side kick seldom scores. However, an opening may be found and exploited by coming from an angle. This is usually achieved by advancing the front foot in your open-sided direction while adjusting for distance. After placing the front foot in its new position, move your rear foot near the front foot and proceed with a rising heel kick with the front foot, a side punch with the hand on the same side as the faking foot, or a front or roundhouse kick with the other foot. This type of move is best suited against an opponent who shifts little in defense.

From a same-side-facing position, make a short adjustment for distance and fake with side kick with the front foot. Step down placing the kicking leg on the floor in an inward direction, placing your body weight on that leg. Once again adjust for distance stepping with the rear leg behind the front leg and simultaneously execute a rising heel kick with your front leg. You must bear in mind that your front-guarding arm must be placed to protect your front-facing kidney which has become exposed to the opponent by stepping in the inward direction.

When the opponent steps back so that the front part of his body is not exposed for a direct kicking move, you may make a hook kick on the base of his neck. Make sure your kicking foot is raised high enough to pass over his shoulder. The kick can also be aimed at his ribs. (The hook kick will be explained in detail in Part IX.)

Continuous Side Stepping. This movement consists of two or more steps to the side, chasing the opponent while he is shifting backward to enable you to execute a side kick at the proper distance. To follow the opponent continuously, a number of adjustments for distance can be combined by stepping with the rear foot over the front foot, bringing the rear foot to the front foot, or crossing the rear foot behind the front foot. This is a conservative procedure in which you are less open to counterattack, but it is slow and you might never catch your retreating opponent. On the other hand, a speedy adjustment may continuously be made by stepping first with the front foot in a hopping motion while the rear foot follows traveling straight sideway.

If you find the distance is too great for your kick to score after having cocked your leg, drop the kicking leg to the floor in side stance and step sideway by hopping with the same leg. As your body travels toward the opponent, the same leg comes up once more into the cocked position. If the distance between you and your opponent is now correct, the side kick is delivered with the hopping foot while placing your rear leg on the floor beneath the center of your body. If your opponent detects your threatened side kick move and again retreats, do not kick but step forward again until you can make a successful kick without wasting motion. (Or, instead, you may apply a flying side kick.)

While executing the continuous hopping sideway motions, stop this motion and step forward with your rear foot placing it ahead of the front foot. Then, jump up on your rear foot toward the opponent, simultaneously cocking the front foot (left) and deliver a flying side kick.

● Side Kick as an Instant Counterattack

The side kick is often used as an instant counterattack against many types of kicks and hand attacks because you can reach a long distance target with it and not leave yourself widely open while executing it. As soon as your opponent moves to initiate an attack, you may execute a side kick or a spot-pushing side kick, since once he commits himself to the attack, it will be difficult for him to defend against your counter move with blocks or shifts. You can also catch your opponent with a side-rising kick at a close range while he is in the process of adjusting for distance to attack you. The power of your side kick is multiplied if it is delivered at the moment your opponent shifts his body toward you.

Instant Attack With the Side Thrust Kick. As soon as your opponent moves in to attack you with a hand technique from a same-side-facing position, you can deliver a side thrust kick (or a spot-pushing side kick) with your front foot after cocking your leg to your body. He creates a large opening for your kick as he steps forward to punch you. This type of instant counterattack often scores even against your opponent's roundhouse-kick attack.

Instant Attack with the Side-Rising Kick. As soon as you detect your opponent cocking his hand for a punch following an adjustment for distance in an opposite-side-facing position, you can extend your front foot forward in a rising motion, kicking him before his punching fist reaches you. If the kick is delivered quickly without any warning, it will stop him from shifting forward. This type of instant attack often can be applied against your opponent when he tries to drive you away to follow through with hand attacks, kicks, or flying moves.

Instant Attack With the Flying Side Kick. This attack is made by a flying side kick which is delivered instantly with your front foot after jumping up from a stationary position. Your flying motion results in the shift of your whole body toward your opponent while he is attacking with a kick, instead of your leaning backward or sideway. This type of defense is often applied against the opponent's kicking attack or against his adjustment for distance for a kick and is a very advanced move which requires good timing.

When your opponent shifts his body forward to deliver a kick, you can jump straight up in the air on both of your feet and simultaneously deliver a flying side kick with your front foot. Try to make the jump from a stationary position to avoid wasting a moment. While you are returning to the floor, guard yourself with your arms or prepare for a combination attack with your hands.

19 Defense Against the Side Kick

THERE are many ways to defend against side kick attacks. Arm blocks are the most important basic defenses and must be perfected as counters against side kicks. Body shifts are often used, both singly and in combination with arm blocks. You must shift backward, forward, or sideway as soon as your opponent initiates his adjustment for distance for a side kick, or begins his kicking motion if the side kick is made from a stationary position. Thus, you should be able to control the distance between you and your opponent.

Any simple arm block can provide a good defense against a side-kick attack provided that the block is powerful enough to stop or deflect the kicking leg. The downward and outward low blocks with the front-guarding arm are most frequently used against a side-kick attack, for the kick is usually aimed at the front-facing ribs under the arm. The rising block or inward or outward high blocks are effective against any kick aimed at a higher target. The rising-heel kick is frequently blocked by an inward middle block.

A normal arm guard in a partially sided posture is a good defense against the side-kick attack. Your front-guarding arm should be on the side of your body protecting the rib cage. Your front and rear feet should be quite close, so you will be able to shift your body quickly. The front foot should be relaxed so it may be lifted up quickly for both defensive and offensive purposes, enabling fast spot shifting to be effectively used against your opponent's initial attacking move.

● Simple Defense and Counterattack

The basic defensive moves against side-kick attacks are the same as those used against any other means of attack. Therefore, this section will cover only those defensive moves which have not yet been fully explained or which are especially used for defense against a side-kick attack. The defensive moves will be explained in conjunction with counterattack moves, so free fighters will not limit their moves to simple defense alone, but will try to create openings for their counterattacks, in order to obtain the maximum advantage from each situation.

Arm-Pulling Block (Pahl Dahngkyu Makgi). This is a defensive move performed by pulling the upper part of your front-guarding arm toward your front-facing ribs, lowering your forearm slightly so your opponent's side kick aimed at your ribs will hit the arm first. If you catch the opponent's kicking foot under your arm while pulling it close to the ribs, you could deflect it by a short inward or outward block. This type of block is only used to protect the rib area when there is no possibility for a better defense. Since it is a weak block, it should be combined with body shifting.

When your opponent attacks your front-facing ribs with a side thrust kick, defend with an arm-pulling block by pulling your front-guarding arm toward your front-facing ribs, deflecting the kicking leg with an outward low block. Always keep your blocking arm flexible so the block is executed with a short but thrusting movement, with the upper part of the arm squeezing into the rib cage. After combining the block with a short backward shift, you may counterattack him.

Smothering Block. The smothering block against a side-kick attack is performed when the distance between you and the attacker becomes shortened by your stepping forward into a side-facing posture while he is moving toward you to deliver a side kick. As soon as the attacker raises his kicking leg to deliver a side kick or when he makes an initial motion to adjust for distance, you must simultaneously move forward toward him, raising your front leg into a cocked position as if to deliver a side kick and instead block his kicking leg with it. Moreover, even if you are unsuccessful in deflecting his kicking leg, his side kick will be weak and inaccurate because of the proximity created by your smothering move. At this distance, many hand attacks can be applied effectively. This type of defense is often used in free fighting against both simple and continuous side-kick attacks.

When the attacker attempts to deliver a side kick with his front foot in a same-side-facing free-fighting position, raise your front leg with its lower part slightly open and push your whole body forward toward the attacker to deflect his kicking leg with your front foot. The advancing motion of your body is made in a side-facing posture as if you were executing a side kick. As soon as the smothering block is made, counterattack with a palm-heel strike, preferably placing your front arm to guard against a possible back-fist punch with his front arm.

Leg Block (*Dahri Ohllyu-makgi*). This block is performed against a side-kick attack by raising your front knee so the lower leg covers the middle and low target areas which directly face the attacker. In addition, you may also raise and pull your front-guarding arm to cover your high target area, so the front-facing area of your entire body is protected against the attacker's double or combination attacks. However, trainees are advised not to use this block too often in free fighting, unless there is no other choice. Reliance on this type of block keeps the trainees from perfecting other defensive moves and, furthermore, it seldom creates an opportunity for counterattack. In addition, this type of defense does not adequately cover all the vital points of your body.

In an opposite-side-facing free-fighting position, block the attacker's side-rising kick with your front leg by raising the knee and pulling it toward you as if you are cocking it to deliver a side kick. Simultaneously pull your front arm toward your body to protect your high target area. As soon as the attacker's kick is stopped by the leg block, you may counterattack with an outward knife-hand strike with your front hand. This type of block should, however, be applied at a short distance from your attacker so your block can easily stop his kick before it is fully extended.

The leg or smothering blocks are particularly good for stopping the attacker's continuous side stepping while driving you back to execute his side-kick attack. You can apply the blocks as soon as you realize the intent of the attacker's continuous stepping, by suddenly stopping your backward shift or changing the shifting course forward as soon as the attacker returns his front leg to the floor to make another hopping movement. Following the stop, you usually find good openings for counterattacking with the hands.

● Counter Shifting

Counter shifting is highly recommended as a counter against the side-kick attack, because it utilizes both defensive and offensive moves. Since your attacker's side-facing posture in which his side kick is executed does not leave much opening for your instant counterattack, you should defend with body shifting and then look for an opening to counterattack as soon as your opponent completes his initial side kick.

While you free fight with counter-shifting moves, you usually avoid your opponent's combination attacks and, at the same time, create an immediate opening for your counterattack while the attacker is off guard. However, the defense is always made easier and you are left in a better position to counterattack when arm blocks are combined with body shifting. The long-distance body shift may be successfully applied to your defensive shifting against a side-kick attack without the use of arm blocks. But, in order to practice the combined defense of arm block and body shifting described in this section, spot shifting, which covers a short distance and is the most flexible means of changing your body's moving direction, is applied to most of the situations below.

Straight Back and Forth Shifting for a Side Kick. This is a defense executed by shifting straight back from the attacker's initial side-kick attack and then counterattacking him with your side kick while shifting your body forward. A flying side kick can also be applied as a counterattack. This type of counterattack can be applied against any type of attack. You can combine the downward or outward low block made with your front arm while spot shifting.

When your opponent attacks with a fast side kick with a hopping adjustment for distance and his kicking leg comes close to you while you are shifting straight backward, you must combine a downward low block with your shift. Then, make a sudden change of moving direction by shifting forward toward the opponent and counterattack with a side thrust kick with your front foot. You usually will catch your opponent off balance.

Step Back and Shift for a Hook Kick. You can defend against your opponent's side-kick attack by shifting one step backward and making an inward middle block, which usually creates openings for counterattacks with hand techniques and kicks.

When your opponent attacks the ribs on your left side with a side thrust kick in a same-side-facing position, you can shift one step back, simultaneously blocking the kicking leg with an inward middle block with your right arm. You can then counterattack with a hook kick with your left foot, pivoting your right foot and pointing the toes slightly to the left. If the distance between you and your opponent becomes quite close following the arm block, you can proceed with the same counter moves but instead execute a backward left elbow attack against the front of the opponent's body or a *Shooto* strike on his neck.

120 Degrees Open Shifting for a Front Kick. The open shifting can be applied against any kicking attack. The shift should preferably cover a long distance, because the revolving of the body usually slows down the sideway shift, leaving the front of the body unprotected. Body shifting in a wide angle usually provides a safer defense against a side thrust kick which usually reaches a long distance in a straight forward direction. However, following a successful defense by open shifting against a side-kick attack, you can counterattack with a front kick, side kick, roundhouse kick, flying kick, and many different hand attacks.

As soon as your opponent starts to make a side thrust kick from an opposite-side-facing position, make an open shift in a wide degree angle, pushing your body weight slightly backward with your front foot (right), simultaneously shifting it toward your right side with your rear foot. You are now in a free-fighting position to the right of your original position. Then, you can counterattack immediately with a front-thrust kick, shifting your body toward your opponent, or you can proceed with your counterattack following an adjustment for distance if the distance between you and your opponent is too great for an immediate counterattack.

Closed Shifting for a Rising-Heel Kick. This type of defense is not often used in free fighting but can be effectively applied against the attacker who frequently commits himself to a simple side thrust kick attack. Since the shifting occurs in a tight position, an arm guard must always protect the front-facing ribs which, while shifting, directly face the attacker. However, an outward low block deflecting the attacker's kicking leg, accompanied by a closed shift, creates an opening for an immediate counterattack with a reverse middle punch, palm-heel strike, hook kick, or rising-heel kick from close range.

When your opponent attacks you with a fast side thrust kick, you can defend with a closed shift preferably performed by moving both feet to your right side, simultaneously making an outward low block to deflect his kicking leg if it comes close to you. You must be particularly alert for an attack against your front kidney, since it is most vulnerably exposed. Then you can counterattack with a rising-heel kick or a side kick after an appropriate adjustment for distance. If the distance remains close after your defensive moves, you can counterattack with hand moves or a hook kick with your right foot instead.

● Immediate Counter Punch With a Smothering Move

A side kick or a rising-heel kick usually requires a certain distance to be effectively executed. If your opponent habitually adjusts for distance in order to initiate his kick, you can defend by shifting slightly forward to smother him so that the distance between you and your opponent will be too short for the kicking leg to be fully extended. Make sure that your opponent does not expect such a shifting move from you before he executes his kick, because he can easily score with his immediate hand attack accompanied by a side fake kick or with a side kick which is delivered following a faking motion without actual adjustment for distance. In general, your defense against a side or rising-heel kick should be such that it is undetectable. Instead of defending always with a shifting away move, such a move of smothering him to take advantage of his adjustment for distance sometimes confuses him so that he cannot easily detect your whereabouts by the time his kick is fully executed.

As soon as your opponent adjusts for distance to deliver a side or rising heel kick, advance forward toward him in a side-facing posture, guarding your front-facing area tightly with your front arm to stop or deflect his kicking leg. Then, deliver an immediate counterattack with your reverse middle punch on his kidney. Your advancing move must begin simultaneously with his adjusting move and it must result in considerable shortening of the distance between you and your opponent. Be sure that you do not move into his kick. Note that your upper body is preferably leaning slightly backward while smothering his adjustment for distance so that you can avoid any accident of rushing into his kick with your face when the kick is aimed at your high target area.

If you notice any sign of the attacking opponent's hand attack which may be delivered immediately following his unsuccessful kick, you must block the attack or guard against it first and deliver a fast counter punch. Sometimes, you can shift into him stopping his kicking leg with your front leg and guarding his hand attack with your front arm, simultaneously delivering a counter punch. A hand attack which the opponent delivers after realizing the ineffectiveness of his kick usually cannot reach you before you score with an immediate counter punch. However, make a habit of blocking such hand attacks even if you score first. This type of move is also good against his simultaneous attack of the kick and punch.

20 When the Kicking Leg Is Grabbed

ONE of the disadvantages of using the side thrust and rising heel kicks in free fighting is that the kicking leg is often grabbed by the opponent and you are then forced off balance or fall down completely. Any kick executed with a snapping motion is seldom grabbed because of the speed with which the leg returns to the cocked position after the kick is delivered. A front kick, for example, is sometimes grabbed, but the good balance retained with the kick and the combined punches or strikes which should immediately follow the kick should not allow the opponent to gain an advantage.

Re-Cocking the Kicking Leg Against a Grab. When the kicking leg is grabbed, pull the leg instantly back to the cocked position in a sharp motion to get it away from the grab, and instantly push it down so the kicking foot touches the supporting knee. Your upper body must lean forward toward the opponent while re-cocking the grabbed leg to your body. The mastery of re-cocking the leg to your body will enable you to retain balance and coordination, therefore you can take advantage of the situation even if it is still being held in his

hands. The distance becomes shortened when you pull your leg back to the cocked position, resulting either in the opponent being pulled forward to you with the grabbed leg or in your being pulled toward the opponent if he stands firm and holds tight. In this proximity to your opponent, you can use your front-guarding arm to attack his high target area or to grab his holding arm to keep safely balanced and simultaneously attack with your other hand.

The supporting knee must remain bent to provide a flexible adjustment against your opponent's pressure on the grabbed leg. If he grabs the kicking leg and moves away from you to make you fall down, your bent knee will help you follow him in long jumping motions by pushing yourself forward with your supporting leg so the distance is shortened and your opponent caught. The importance of leaning forward with the upper body must be stressed when the kicking leg is being pulled back and down. This will enable you to follow the opponent in a tightly set position rather than be dragged. You should grab the opponent's front-guarding arm or shoulder as soon as the distance is sufficiently shortened by your pulling motion and press him down simultaneously with hand attacks to avoid being dragged. Never lean backward when your kicking leg is grabbed.

When the opponent lifts up your grabbed leg strongly to throw you, you can defend better when in a front-facing posture. The side-facing posture from which the side kick is made is not strong enough to enable you to move with agility, even if the grabbed leg is pulled back to the cocked position. You must get used to twisting your body outward in order for you to face the opponent straight forward while pulling the grabbed leg back to its cocked position. Your defensive move against the opponent's grab should be made as soon as your kicking leg is grabbed.

In order to pull the grabbed left leg back to the cocked position in a side-facing posture, first pull it back, bending the kicking knee. Simultaneously twist the leg to the left with your upper body twisting in the same direction. While pressing it, lean forward. The whole move of pulling, pivoting, twisting, and leaning must be done with a fast speedy motion. You can combine this motion with fast hand attacks while the opponent is engaged in holding your leg.

Twisting the Grabbed Leg. When you grab your opponent's kicking leg, you may try to lift up the leg or move away holding it. However, there are a couple of excellent ways to unbalance your opponent. As soon as you seize the kicking foot, pull it away from the opponent's body to prevent him from cocking it back and simultaneously twist it outward. Once it is twisted the opponent cannot easily pull it back to the cocked position and, moreover, he might fall down as a result of the twisting motion of his leg.

In order to twist the opponent's kicking right leg, hold his foot with both hands, the toes with the left hand and the heel with the right. As soon as you hold it this way, pull it toward you and twist it to your left quickly, holding both your hands close to your body. The sharp twist will drop the opponent on the floor. It could, however, result in injury to his joints.

Pulling the Grabbed Leg. Pull your opponent's leg to pass it alongside the front of your body as soon as you grab it, and attack with a punch while your opponent is being pulled forward and off guard. When this action is performed instantly without a wasted moment, your opponent finds no chance to recover from the situation, even if his leg is already halfway cocked to his own body. This is one of the safest and most expedient ways to turn this situation to your advantage and is therefore highly recommended to trainees for application in free fighting. It is comparatively safe to practice in the classroom.

Pull the grabbed leg toward you with both hands, passing it in front of your body. You may raise it slightly while pulling. Attack with a reverse punch as soon as the leg is dropped, guarding with your front arm against the opponent's possible back-fist strike.

You must pull the leg in front of you, and not to your back. However, when the situation arises, it is possible to pull it with a simple backward stepping motion.

After grabbing the leg, pull it slightly toward your left side first, and turn your body to the left, holding his leg close to your body. As soon as you step back with his leg in your hands, push it away with your right hand and simultaneously execute a kick to his kidney following an adjustment for distance if necessary.

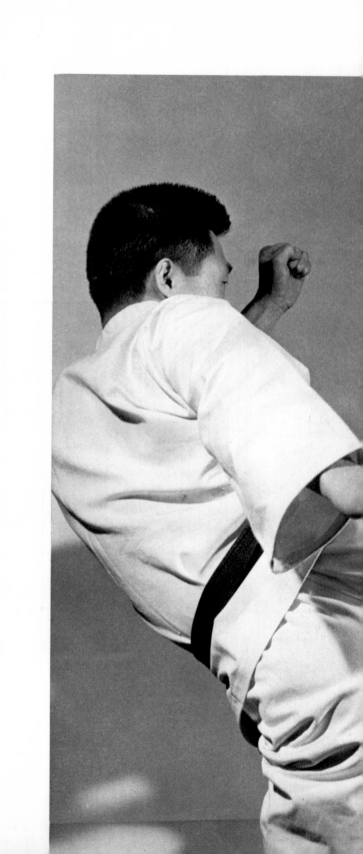

21 How to Make the Roundhouse Kick

THE ROUNDHOUSE KICK is one of the most advanced movements. It can be used in free fighting as either a surprise or finishing attack. Trainees who have no difficulty with the front and side kicks can easily learn to make the roundhouse kick. It is generally made with a snapping motion of the kicking knee in an arc parallel to the floor, moving from the side of the body to the front. The swinging motion of the hip while delivering the kick is different from the hip movements used in front and side kicks. As in the front kick, the striking surface of the roundhouse kick is the ball of the foot, and its targets are the kidneys and most of the high and middle areas of the front part of the body.

If you overswing your hip toward your opponent while delivering the kick, it causes the entire body to rotate, and you lose your balance. The body advancement occurring during weight shifting is usually slower while delivering a roundhouse kick than in the front kick. The toes of your kicking foot can be injured unless the kick is correctly delivered; therefore, the kick is sometimes made with the instep of the foot, after flexing the ankle downward.

● Roundhouse Snap Kick (*Tohllyu Cha-pusugi*)

The roundhouse snap kick is made with the snapping motion of the kicking knee moving in an arc parallel to the floor while the upper body is twisted against the kicking direction. This kick is not a killing technique but transmits a shocking impact to the target, enabling the kicker to maintain good balance. The upper part of the body is usually in a front-facing posture, and the kicking force is achieved by the snapping knee motion.

To make a roundhouse snap kick with your rear foot in forward stance, first cock the kicking leg, lifting it up on your side so that the lower part of the leg is parallel to the floor. The ankle of the kicking leg must be fully flexed and the toes curled up. Then, deliver the kick in a circular motion, the lower part of the leg traveling parallel to the floor while slightly swinging the hip and pivoting the supporting foot to the left, and finally snapping the knee. You must keep good balance, so you can pull the kicking leg back to the original cocked position and return it to the floor. You must not stand on the toes or heel while delivering the kick.

● Roundhouse Thrust Kick (*Tohllyu Cha-tzirugi*)

The roundhouse thrust kick is a finishing kick, with its power generated from the rotating motion of the whole body, as well as from the snapping motion of the kicking knee. As with any other type of thrust kick, the kicker will find it difficult to control his balance following the roundhouse thrust kick. Therefore his arms must always be placed to continue with a fast combination attack or to block the opponent's counterattack while he is in an unbalanced position. The upper body posture must be in about a half-front-facing direction at the execution of the kick. The rotation of the body beyond that point may unbalance the kicker completely.

In order to deliver a roundhouse thrust kick in forward or side stance, cock the kicking leg on your side in the same way as in the roundhouse snap kick. Then, execute the kick, extending the kicking leg in an arc, traveling parallel to the floor, simultaneously pivoting the supporting foot and swinging the hips. The whole body rotates to the left. The rotation of your body must be stopped at or before the direct body line, so you can maintain either a side or a half-front-facing posture in a side or low stance after the kicking leg returns to the floor.

● Short Roundhouse Kick (*Pahn Tohllyu-chagi*)

The short roundhouse kick is made with the kicking leg traveling in a short, circular arc which simultaneously rises to the height of the target. The cocked position of the kicking leg is somewhere between the kicker's front and side, and the power of the kick is generated from the sharp rising and short circular motion of its delivery. Except for this, the execution of the short roundhouse kick is identical to that of the long roundhouse snap or thrust kick. This type of short kick often can be made with the front foot. It takes less body maneuvering but is weaker in power than the long kicks. The striking surface is the instep or ball of the foot.

To make a short roundhouse kick with your front foot in back stance, cock the kicking leg, slightly pressing your kicking knee inward and the kicking foot outward, placing it off to your side in front of your hip. Then, deliver the kick by first raising the leg and kicking sharply inward as the leg is about to reach the target.

● Flying Roundhouse Kick (*Dtuiyu Tohllyu-chagi*)

The flying roundhouse kick can be either a long or a short kick delivered from the air. Body twisting is very pronounced in this kick, and the balance becomes weaker as the rotation of the body increases. Therefore, trainees more often use the short roundhouse kick. The flying roundhouse kick is best applied in free fighting from an oblique direction for a simple initial attack or a counterattack following an open shifting defense. It can be made by jumping up and kicking with the same foot or by jumping up with one foot and kicking with the other.

Jumping and Kicking With the Same Foot. To make a flying round-house kick with your rear foot in forward stance, step forward placing your right foot at an angle to your right side. Then, jump up with the right leg, pulling it up into the cocked position, and deliver the kick while rotating your body to the left. At the moment of impact, your body must be twisted to maintain balance.

Jumping on One Foot and Kicking With the Other. In order to make a flying roundhouse kick with your rear foot in forward stance, jump up with your front foot while cocking the kicking leg on your right side. At the height of the target, slightly rotate your body to the left and simultaneously deliver the kick with a snapping motion of your kicking knee. Return to the floor after bringing the kicking leg back to your body. Generally, an adjustment for distance provides an advancing motion for the jump.

22 How to Use the Roundhouse Kick

THE ROUNDHOUSE KICK can be applied as a surprise attack against an opponent who carelessly leaves an opening which can be reached from an oblique direction. With the roundhouse kick you can effectively attack the front part of the body of those who defend their side by using arm guards without using many actual arm blocks. When your opponent defends with an arm-pulling block against your side-kick attack, for example, you can attack his front with a roundhouse kick with your other foot.

The roundhouse kick requires a big body maneuver, so your kick is often noticed by the opponent before it is fully executed. Since the kick is delivered in an oblique direction, the front part of your body is sometimes directly open to your opponent's instant counterattack. As a whole, body balance causes the most difficulty in applying the roundhouse kick to free fighting. You must always be careful not to overcommit the whole body while delivering this kick. Therefore, many free fighters use the roundhouse kick as a secondary move in a combination attack, rather than as an initial attacking move.

● Basics for Roundhouse-Kick Application

The basics of positions and adjustment for distance in applying roundhouse kicks to free fighting are identical to those of the front and side kicks which have previously been covered. You can easily make a short roundhouse kick with your front foot from cat stance and back stance, but the kick will be weak in power. A strong and finishing roundhouse kick is usually made with the rear foot from any stance, but long-distance stances such as forward stance and side stance will add more force to the kick. You may use the type of roundhouse kick that best suits the particular situation, following a proper adjustment for distance in an adequately guarded position.

Placement of Arms While Delivering the Roundhouse Kick. While delivering a roundhouse kick your front arm is usually held behind the kicking leg, for this helps twist your body for balance. Especially in the roundhouse thrust kick, in which your balance becomes weak because of the body rotation, such an arm placement will enable you to use your front arm for an inward arm block against a defender's counterattack punch or for a fast punch before he can make a counter move after your kick. The other arm should be held to guard the front part of your body or brought outward in the same direction as the front arm to aid the body in twisting.

When your roundhouse thrust kick aimed at your opponent's kidney is blocked, and your body is overcommitted to the kick thereby preventing you from shifting away from his counter moves, you must try to take the best advantage of the situation. Drop your kicking leg on the floor, preferably in side stance, and simultaneously make an inward middle block with either arm against his counter punch. If your opponent is still in a defensive position when you are in side stance following your roundhouse kick, you can make a hand attack with the front arm instead of a defensive block.

● Roundhouse Kick and Following Attacks

As with any other kick, you may combine many hand attacks and kicks following a roundhouse kick. The roundhouse kick and side kick, the roundhouse snap kick and front kick, or two or more roundhouse snap kicks can be combined and applied to free fighting. Against the opponent who frequently defends by body shifting, you can start your move with a roundhouse fake kick to either adjust for distance or to apply other attacks. The flying roundhouse kick should be applied from an oblique direction after driving your opponent backward, or by following him when he defends by shifting to his side.

Roundhouse Kick and Hand Attacks. You can apply a roundhouse kick to free fighting in combination with the straight side punch, palm-heel attack, or knife-hand strike whenever you are close to your opponent but not in immediate danger from his counterattack.

When your roundhouse kick is double arm blocked and your opponent is not in a position to deliver an immediate counterattack, you can step down into forward stance without bringing the kicking leg back to your body. Then, simultaneously, deliver a palm-heel attack with your front hand to an open target area of his body.

If your opponent arm blocks your palm-heel attack, you may attack his solar plexus with a fast front snap kick with your front foot while shifting your weight backward.

Roundhouse Thrust Kick and the Rising-Heel Kick. When your opponent defends with body shifting against your roundhouse thrust kick thereby causing you to lose your balance, you can initiate a continuous attack with a rising-heel kick with your rear foot. This combination move is particularly effective against the opponent's counter-shifting attack. A roundhouse fake kick can always replace the thrust kick as a method of adjusting for distance or creating openings, or it can be combined with the rising-heel kick. The application of the roundhouse fake kick is identical to that of the front and side fake kicks.

When your opponent defends with body shifting against your roundhouse thrust kick and tries to take advantage of your unbalanced position, you may quickly proceed with another attack or a rising-heel kick with your rear foot. You can often score with the heel kick when your opponent makes a counter move against you, or when he carelessly leaves himself open, believing you are too unbalanced to make a combination attack.

Instead of the combination attack with the rising-heel kick, you may proceed with a hook kick with your left foot while rotating your body around. This type of combination kick is particularly effective when your opponent attempts to counterattack you in a side-facing posture. (See Part IX for the hook kick.)

Roundhouse Fake for a Side Kick. This type of fake move is often advised against an opponent who immediately responds to your simple initial attacking move with an arm block, or with an immediate counter punch, lacking in body shifting. However, this move can be vulnerable against the opponent's instant counterattack with a side kick or a straight forward fist punch.

In a same-side-facing position, you can rotate your body with your rear leg cocked for a roundhouse kick, faking your opponent into defending against a roundhouse kick which you do not really plan to execute. As soon as your body rotates to where the cocked leg points directly to the target then extend it out directly toward your opponent, delivering the kick with the heel part of the foot. The motion of your body rotation must be stopped, and the direction of the kicking force is immediately changed from a circular one for a roundhouse kick to one straight forward for a side kick.

When your opponent habitually defends against your roundhouse kick with one step or simple body shifting, you can reach him with a spot-pushing side kick immediately following a roundhouse fake move. This type of attack scores successfully when the opponent does not expect your spot-pushing kick.

If your opponent shifts one step back against your roundhouse fake kick, you can proceed with a spot-pushing side kick. The spot-pushing kick often scores effectively when its execution is made before the faking motion is completed. In other words, both kicks should be delivered as if they are one simple unit move. A spot-pushing hook kick can be combined with the fake kick in case your body has rotated too far along with the faking leg. Prepare for a combination attack with the hands in case the kicking leg is grabbed.

● Roundhouse Kick Following Other Moves

A roundhouse kick is frequently applied in free fighting as a finishing kick following various punches, kicks, or fake moves.

Deflecting the Guarding Arm and the Roundhouse Kick. In order to avoid the danger of an instant counterattack from your opponent while delivering a roundhouse kick with your rear foot, you may deflect your opponent's front-guarding arm with your front arm before you execute the kick. This deflection also can be an effective fake creating an opening for the roundhouse kick. You can also apply the roundhouse kick following a simple back-fist attack, an outward knife-hand strike with your front arm, or a faking motion of such hand attacks.

In order to deliver a roundhouse kick with your rear foot in a same-side-facing position, you may first make a surprise move by deflecting your opponent's front-guarding arm with your front arm, so that he reacts to your hand move. Simultaneously, cock your rear foot and deliver a fast roundhouse kick.

When the deflection is made to create an opening for a roundhouse kick, it should be accompanied by an adjustment for distance so the kicking leg can be cocked first and delivered in a large arc for increased power. In addition, a fake punch with your rear fist following the deflection usually provides a forward momentum to the rear side of your body, thus a roundhouse kick with the rear foot can be executed easily.

Side-Rising Kick and the Roundhouse Thrust Kick. If you make an unsuccessful attempt to execute a side-rising kick, you may find yourself at an appropriate distance for a roundhouse thrust kick with your opposite leg by stepping forward after returning the kicking leg to side or low stance.

When your side-rising kick is defended in combination with a short body shift, you should first return your kicking leg forward in side stance to adequately guard your front-facing area against your opponent's immediate counterattacks. You can continue shifting your weight slightly forward in side stance so that your rear leg becomes free of weight. Then, you can cock the kicking leg and deliver a roundhouse thrust kick with a quick rotation of your body if there is no immediate danger of counterattack from the opponent.

Front Fake Kick and the Short Roundhouse Kick. When your opponent mainly defends with arm blocks or short body shifts, you might be able to create an opening for a short roundhouse kick with the same leg that first makes a front fake kick. The short roundhouse kick is usually weak in power, but if accurately placed on a vital point, it can be totally effective. It is a surprise move in which the kicking direction unexpectedly changes from straight forward to an arc, and the target changes from the solar plexus to the head.

Maintain a good balance as you execute the fake kick by not committing your body weight toward your opponent. As soon as the kicking foot is cocked back to your body, rotate your body slightly to the left and simultaneously arc out for a short roundhouse kick to his head. This surprise move will be very hard to block unless your opponent is very experienced and is expecting such a move.

23 Defense Against the Roundhouse Kick

THE APPLICATION of basic defensive moves against the roundhouse kick attack is identical to that of front- and side-kick attacks. In general, you can defend in various ways using the simple arm block, body shifting, counter shifting, instant counterattack, the combination of an arm block and body shift, and the arm block with body twisting. Defense is always safer from a side-facing posture because it does not leave enough room for an opponent's roundhouse kick to strike you without hitting your front-guarding arm first, unless his kick is delivered from an oblique direction. Furthermore, it does not leave much opening for his combination attack. Since the execution of the opponent's roundhouse kick requires him to make a heavy body maneuver, you might find excellent opportunities for counterattack following your successful defense. Unlike the other kicks previously covered, the roundhouse kick attack can be easily thwarted by a fast, short, and snappy move.

Defense with body shifting, which is one of the most important defensive techniques of free fighting, has already been covered in earlier parts of this book, but some of its characteristic applications to the roundhouse-kick attack will be covered in this section. Any roundhouse kick aimed at a target higher than the kidney or solar plexus should be blocked with middle or high blocks.

● Inward Arm Block

Against a roundhouse kick aimed at the front part of your body, an inward arm block for both the middle and high target areas is the preferred defense, with your body in a side-facing posture. The circle-stepping move can be effectively combined with this type of arm block for a doubly safe defense.

As soon as you detect the initiation of your opponent's roundhouse thrust kick, guard your open target area by moving your rear foot slightly in a counter-clockwise direction, at the same time making an inward middle block, using your front arm with its elbow close to your solar plexus. You may also use the same arm to block the opponent's following hand attack, or you can deliver a fast straight reverse punch from your left side while extending the front foot forward in a right-side angle, moving your upper body away from his possible combination hand attack.

● Double-Arm Block

Double-arm blocks can be made in downward, outward, or inward directions with the front-guarding arm, while the other arm covers the front of the body. Both arms should be used to defend with maximum safety against a strong, killing attack. The double-arm block should be made in a side-facing posture against a roundhouse-kick attack.

When your opponent executes a roundhouse thrust kick toward the midsection of your front body, defend with a double-arm block by making an inward middle block with your front-guarding arm and placing your rear arm tightly under the front elbow. The rear arm can be easily moved for another block or counter punch. Then, you may counterattack with a palm-heel strike with your rear hand to the opponent's chin, simultaneously extending your front leg forward for body advancement. Meanwhile, your front-guarding arm must be ready to defend against his potential hand attacks. You could make a short back-fist punch with the front arm following your double-arm block before making the palm-heel strike.

● Arm and Leg Block

Often, instead of a double-arm block, a defense is made which combines a leg block with an inward arm block. The arm and leg block is used only when you are unable to shift away from the attacking opponent's fast roundhouse kick, since it is no more than a guarding block, placing you in a weak position to defend against the opponent's combination attacks. Furthermore, this block does not allow you much opportunity for counterattack. However, you might sometimes find yourself in a situation where you must first make a temporary block with your arm and leg to guard your body against your opponent's instant round-house-kick counterattack, which is executed when you initiate attacking moves with a fake kick or an adjustment for distance.

While you are moving forward with an adjustment for distance to execute a short round-house kick to your opponent in an opposite-side-facing position, you might sometimes en-counter a fast, short roundhouse kick executed as an instant counterattack. As soon as you find that your initial kick cannot be delivered before his counter kick reaches you, you must block his kick by first rotating your body inward, cocking your front leg for a leg block and then making an inward high block with your front-guarding arm. His roundhouse kick will be stopped either by your leg block or your arm block. If you find an opening following this block, you can make a side thrust kick with the blocking leg in order to prevent him from initiating a combination attack.

When the opponent's roundhouse kick is blocked with your leg, the shin of your blocking leg often collides with his shin. Therefore, this type of block is only recommended when there is no other alternative. However, this type of injury must be expected in free fighting when you defend with just blocks and do not use body shifting.

● Defense With Body Shifting

Defense with body shifting is always effective, since you can easily control the distance between you and your opponent to avoid combined moves following his roundhouse-kick attack. As with the defense against the side kick, you will be much safer against your opponent's roundhouse kick when you defend with a combination of spot shifting and an arm block. You might be able to score very well with counter shifting against your opponent's initial attack, because the roundhouse kick is usually executed with a large body maneuver and frequently results in poor coordination.

The open body shift against a roundhouse kick aimed at the front part of your body can be utilized as effectively as against any other kicking attack, because you can shift quickly to one side when the kick is executed toward you in an arc from the opposite side. For the same reason, body shifting backward is highly recommended against any type of roundhouse kick attack. Frequently, you might be able to create openings for your counterattack following a defense by a simple backward shift.

Assuming that your opponent attacks you with a roundhouse thrust kick in a same-side-facing position, you can defend against the kick by making an open shift. While shifting, move your front foot to a point on your right side at a wide angle. Then, counterattack with a roundhouse kick with your rear foot. (Instead, you may counterattack with a front kick with your rear foot, or a side kick with the front foot.) If the distance is too great following your defensive shift, you must counterattack with kicks or punches accompanied by an offensive shift.

● Instant Counterattack Against the Roundhouse Kick

Since the body maneuver involved in executing a roundhouse kick takes longer than in most other kicks, you may sometimes apply a side thrust kick, back-fist punch, or side punch as an instant counterattack, delivered at the moment your opponent initiates his kick. Besides, when your opponent is kicking in an arc from his side, his front-facing area is usually left directly vulnerable to your instant counterattack. You can reach farther with a side thrust kick or a rising heel kick than with other means of instant counterattacks.

As soon as you detect your opponent's roundhouse-kick attack with his rear foot in a same-side-facing position, you can instantly counterattack with a side thrust kick. First, adjust for distance by bringing your rear foot slightly forward in a hopping motion and then deliver a side thrust kick with your front foot toward the front part of your opponent's body before his kick reaches you. Your body must be in a side-facing posture, preferably with your arms guarding the front part of your body while kicking.

Sometimes, your instant counterattack can be made from a slightly oblique direction following an adjustment for distance, by bringing the rear foot forward to an angle on the left side, with your arms guarding the front part of your body. The adjustment for distance must be made in a small but fast hopping motion.

Part
IX Other Kicks

24 Knee Kick (*Moohrup Chagi*)

THE KNEE KICK, like the elbow attack, is a short attack utilized as an offensive move in free fighting. The striking surface is the upper portion of the knee, usually delivered with a thrusting motion. In general, there are two types of knee kicks: the front knee kick which is delivered straight forward; and the roundhouse knee kick which is delivered in a circular motion from your side to your front. However, because of the short distance the kick travels, the kicking power must be transmitted directly from the body while raising the kicking knee forward for the front-knee kick and while swinging the hips in a circular motion for the roundhouse-knee kick. The main target of the kick is the groin, but it can also be used to attack the middle and high target areas in free fighting.

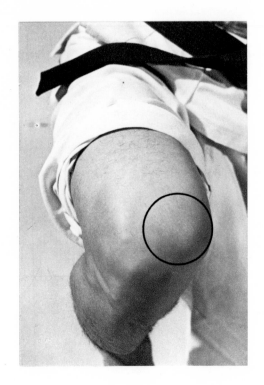

Front-Knee Kick. To make a front-knee kick in forward stance with your rear leg, cock the kicking leg with the knee slightly downward and the lower leg bent tightly back against the thigh. Then, raise your knee upward while slightly pushing your hip forward. End by lowering the kicking leg forward in another forward stance.

The front-knee kick can also be made by just raising the knee straight up in an uppercut motion. This is easy to make and also strong when it is applied to your opponent's groin or to his head while pressing it downward with your hands.

Roundhouse-Knee Kick. Assuming forward stance to make a round-house-knee kick with your right knee, first cock the kicking leg on your side with the lower leg bent tightly back against the thigh and the upper leg parallel to the floor, extended almost to your right side. Then, deliver the kick in a circular motion to the imaginary target on your front by pivoting the supporting foot and swinging the hips slightly to your left, while twisting your body to your right in order to retain balance.

When to Use the Knee Kick. The knee kick can be applied at close range following either a crash or arm block in free fighting. When the distance does not allow the execution of effective kicks, and both you and your opponent are guarding against hand attacks, you might score with an unexpected knee-kick attack. Kicking groin or head targets must not be applied against another trainee but practiced only as a self-defense move, since its application can result in severe injury. However, the roundhouse-knee kick can sometimes score on the middle target area in free fighting.

Assuming that your opponent adjusts for distance in order to execute a back-fist punch with his front hand in a same-side-facing position, you can defend with an inward arm block. Following the block, you can grab and try to pull his punching hand in order to unbalance him, thus preventing a possible second punch with his other hand. While both of you are in this position, you may try a sudden roundhouse-knee kick to his solar plexus.

25 Stamping Kick (Naeryu Chagi)

THE STAMPING KICK is applied both as an offensive and defensive move, delivered against the opponent's knee, shin, ankle, and other vital low target areas. The stamping kick can be used to attack the opponent on the front, back, and sides with either the heel or the outer edge of the foot. It is made with a thrusting motion. The kick can be effectively applied to most parts of the lower leg in free fighting, for the opponent cannot block low enough with his arms without losing balance. A serious injury on the knee joint or on the ankle can often result from injudicious use of the stamping kick unless it is completely controlled.

From left above: Front stamping kick with the heel, front stamping kick with the edge, back stamping kick with the heel, back stamping kick with the edge, right-side stamping kick with the heel, right-side stamping kick with the edge, left-side stamping kick with the heel, left-side stamping kick with the edge.

To practice a stamping kick in forward stance with your rear foot, cock the kicking leg by raising the knee close to the chest. For a heel kick, the ankle must be flexed upward with the heel down and thrust to the imaginary target in the front, back, or on the sides. For the side edge kick, your kicking foot must be cocked in the same way as the side kick by flexing the ankle upward, turning the toes slightly inward and the heel outward, and simultaneously thrusting the side edge of the foot down. As soon as the kick is completed, bring the kicking leg back to its original cocked position before returning it to the floor. Your supporting knee must always remain bent to provide good balance while executing the kick.

When to Use the Kick. You can attack most of the low parts of your opponent's body with the stamping kick while he is in free-fighting position as well as any other weak spots when he is down on the floor. You can sometimes combine a hand attack with this kick by kicking his knee to make him lose balance when he makes a defensive body shift. The stamping kick with the side edge of the foot can be used effectively in free fighting as an instant counterattack or to stop the opponent's initial attacking moves by kicking his lower leg while he is adjusting for distance or delivering a kick or punch. The stamping fake kick is frequently applied in free fighting to draw the opponent's attention so that you create an opening on him.

As an Initial Attack. You may initiate an attack with the stamping kick against the opponent who defends mainly with arm blocks. The attacking procedure is similar to that of the front or side kick.

To make a stamping kick with the side edge of your front foot in an opposite-side-facing position, adjust for distance and cock the kicking leg to thrust it to the opponent's front-facing knee. Since the cocking position is similar to that of the side kick, your opponent can easily be misled by the cocked position of your kicking leg. A fast adjustment for distance, preferably in a hopping motion, is always advisable in order to catch the opponent off guard and continue your attack with a palm-heel or knife-hand strike. The stamping kick must always be made from a well-balanced position without leaning your upper body too much away from the opponent.

As an Instant Counter Move. The stamping kick can be effectively applied in free fighting as an instant counterattack against an opponent's offense. This counterattack mainly serves to stop the opponent's offense by kicking his front-facing knee or leg while he is adjusting for distance, thereby stopping his forward motion, or by deflecting his kicking leg as he delivers a kick. For a fast counter move, the stamping kick is frequently made with the front foot.

To make a stamping kick with the side edge of your kicking foot against your opponent's initial side-kick attack, bring your front foot toward your body to cock it as soon as you notice your opponent's offensive move. Then, thrust it at your opponent's kicking leg before his kick is fully extended. The front part of your body must be well guarded with your arms while delivering the kick, so you can safely defend against any possible attacks while you are stamp kicking. Be sure to develop the habit of cocking the kicking leg back to your body following the stamping kick unless you are prepared to deliver continuous counterattacks.

As a Fake Kick. The stamping kick can be effectively applied as a fake kick by extending the kicking leg slightly toward the opponent and cocking it back to the body at full speed for another kick. A stamping fake kick followed by a side-rising kick occasionally scores in free fighting against an opponent who defends mainly with his front arm. This type of combination kick is very weak, but is a surprise move which must be completed very quickly before the opponent becomes aware of it.

In an opposite-side-facing position, adjust for distance and make a stamping fake kick with the front foot without thrusting power in it. Cock the kicking leg quickly back to the body line following the fake kick, maintaining strong balance, and simultaneously execute a side-rising kick to your opponent's high target area while he is defending against your stamping fake kick. Both kicks must be delivered quickly, with a snapping motion, as if they were a simple unit attack.

26 Hook Kick

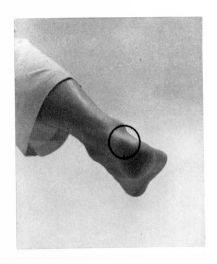

THE HOOK KICK is made with the kicking foot traveling in an arc parallel to the floor. The striking surface is the rear part of the heel. This kick is delivered in the opposite direction from that of the roundhouse kick which was covered in Part VIII. As with the roundhouse kick, the striking area for this kick is the face, back of the head, and most of the middle target area. When it is applied as a self-defense kick, the groin and shin bone would also become vulnerable targets.

While delivering the kick, you must pivot on your supporting foot as your body rotates, otherwise a tremendous strain would occur on the weak spots of the ankle or knee of your supporting leg. For good coordination, your body balance must be well retained. While rotating your body as you kick, special care must be taken to protect your back from the opponent's instant counterattack. Covering your back slightly with your arm by rotating it backward first and then kicking, would be advisable because the arm can guard against and deflect the opponent's instant counterattack; and this also helps to rotate the entire body smoothly.

When to Use the Kick. The hook kick is mainly used as an offensive kick, particularly as a secondary move. Sometimes, it works effectively as a counterattack kick when the opponent does not expect the attack executed in a hooking motion. A side kick or a rising heel kick, which is delivered directly from your body to the striking area, is somewhat similar to this type of kick, whose unusual delivery is accompanied by the motion of body rotation first. This type of an "indirect" kick is hard to block because it is delivered unexpectedly from an unexpected direction.

The hook kick is generally delivered in either of two ways: with the hooking motion of the kicking knee or with the spinning motion of the entire body. The kick in the hooking motion is generally weaker than the one in the spinning motion, but as the former usually allows better coordination and less body maneuvering, it can be more safely applied. The power of this kick should be measured by the degree of the spinning body and balance. This type of kick is hard to control because it is delivered in a thrusting motion, and special care must be taken because you cannot see the target directly while delivering the kick.

Following a Fake Motion. Your hook kick can be effectively applied to the high-section or to the kidney of the defending opponent when he takes for granted that your side kick will come directly to the front-facing area of his body, and he therefore plans to defend by tightening his arm guards to cover the area, or by using an arm and leg block so the kick cannot penetrate. Sometimes, he does not shift far away in order to make a fast counterattack with his reverse forward punch immediately after deflecting or stopping your kicking leg. When you initiate your kick by stepping in a hopping motion in the same manner as if to make a rising heel kick with your front foot, those opponents who are used to arm blocking such a kick can be easily fooled when the kick is delivered from an unexpected direction. The hopping motion of the adjustment for distance, which is similar to that of a rising heel kick or a side kick, makes him prepare to defend against an imaginary kick and to waste his motion, as it turns out to be a faking motion which, as a result, creates an opening on the high-section of the opponent.

This type of kick is not usually strong enough to be a killing blow. However, you can proceed with additional attacking moves when your opponent is thrown off guard or off balance by your kick. The main force of the kick is generated by the twisting motion of your hip and the hooking motion of the kicking knee.

If your opponent responded to your initial attacking move by shifting away and then attempted to make an immediate counter shift, the distance between you and your opponent might be too short for a combination attack with such a long-range kick as a rising heel kick with the same foot. You may then follow through with a hook kick with your rear foot by delivering the kick along with the rotation of your body, deflecting his counter-punching arm or kicking leg with your arm. It is especially worthwhile to try such a combination attack with the hook kick when you are in an unbalanced position following your unsuccessful initial kick, and therefore in a vulnerable situation. Sometimes, you may fake with a side kick with the front foot first and follow through with the hook kick with the other foot to catch the opponent while he is wasting his motion against your initial fake kick. You can aim at the midsection of his body instead.

From an Oblique Direction. When your opponent habitually steps slightly toward you to counter punch while you are initiating an attack, or guards the front part of his body without much body shifting away, you can sometimes catch him with a hook kick which is delivered from his (right) side. Your kicking foot will travel in an arc toward the front-facing area of his face or body. You can put yourself into such a position following an unsuccessful roundhouse thrust kick, roundhouse fake kick, or simply by stepping forward and placing your rear foot to his (right) side.

When you are in an opposite-side-facing position, you can move onto his side by simply extending your front foot forward in an oblique direction and delivering a hook kick with your rear foot. This type of move might be effectively applied against an opponent who would not expect a combination attack from your poorly coordinated position, as long as you can get to his side successfully. Note that your body must be rotated completely to face him directly if you do not wish to stop the kick at the target. Such rotation would increase the thrusting motion of your hook kick thereby making the kick stronger. Even if this type of kick is not as strong as the front kick, side kick, or roundhouse kick, such a thrusting kick, which is hard to control, can still cause damage on a weak spot and it is therefore advisable to aim at the midsection of the body in order to avoid facial injury.

As a Combination Kick. The hook kick is often applied as a secondary move in a combination attack. Some moves that go well with the hook kick are a roundhouse kick with one foot and a hook kick with the other, and punching and kicking with the opposite foot. Sometimes, a hook kick can be combined with sweeping for either defensive or offensive purposes.

If the combination of your sweeping and reverse fist punch does not come out successfully because you happen to loose your own balance following your sweeping motion, you must try to make a hook kick or a back kick with the same leg you used for sweeping. This is an unexpected kick which can be delivered from your uncoordinated position and the idea of this kick is to catch your opponent who is rushing toward you for a counterattack. The rotation of your body to the right for the sweeping and its sudden change to the left for the kick makes it physically impossible for you to thrust strongly with the kick, and hand attacks are always advisable following such a kick.

To execute a strong hook kick as a secondary move, you may first deliver a light sweep (sweeping fake) and then proceed with a hook kick with the front foot following an immediate adjustment for distance.

27 Miscellaneous Kicks

● **Back Kick (*Dui Chagi*)**

The back kick is made by extending the heel of the kicking foot toward an opponent behind you. The targets for this kick are the groin and most of the midsection area. The back kick is delivered with a thrusting rather than snapping motion, and is weak because of the lack of the body advancement while executing it. This kick is generally used as an instant counter kick or a secondary attack following other moves.

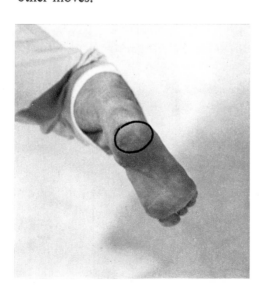

How to Make the Kick. To make a back kick in forward stance with your rear foot, cock the kicking leg by raising its knee to your body line as in the front kick. (You may make the back kick with your front foot instead.) The supporting knee must be slightly bent to retain good balance. The ankle of your kicking foot is flexed upward and your head is turned to the left to watch the opponent while kicking with your left foot. Then, thrust your kicking foot straight backward, with the heel rising slightly upward, and the upper body leaning slightly forward. As soon as the kick is completed, cock the kicking leg back to the body line while straightening your body. Return the kicking foot into forward stance either by stepping forward or backward.

When to Use the Kick. The back kick is mainly used as a surprise attack. You can use the kick as an initial attack for the purpose of self-defense against an opponent who tries to attack from the rear. In karate free fighting, you can apply the back kick as a secondary attack to protect your back from the opponent's counter move after your initial attack has been thwarted. If your opponent rushes toward you to take advantage of your back-facing position, and you cannot find a better defense against his move, you can deliver an instant counterattack with the back kick.

Assume that you make an initial attack with a roundhouse kick, and your opponent defends against the kick with the combination of an arm block and body shift, and plans to counterattack with his hands. As soon as you return your kicking foot to the floor, you can cock the other leg and execute a back kick. Because such an instant counter kick is an unexpected move, the opponent can often be caught with it while he is wide open. Make sure that you watch the opponent before the kick is delivered in order to attack with accuracy. Then, you may return to a well-guarded free-fighting position with good balance. You can also start your initial kicking move with a side or a roundhouse fake kick.

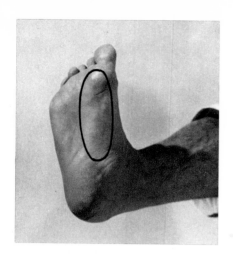

● Crescent Kick

The crescent kick is seldom used in free fighting, but it can occasionally be used for both defensive and offensive purposes when the situation arises. The striking surface is the sole of the kicking foot, and it is made in a circular arc similar to a roundhouse kick. The crescent kick is a weak attack because the striking surface is not sharp enough to concentrate the kicking force.

How to Make the Kick. To make a crescent kick in forward stance with your right foot, first cock your right knee. The position of the cocked leg is similar to that of the front kick except the leg is held in an oblique direction somewhere between your front and right side. Then, open the knee to raise the kicking foot and simultaneously deliver the kick in a circular motion to your left, by swinging the hips while twisting your body. The kicking foot must be stopped in front of you, and cocked back by bringing it straight to your body.

When to Use the Kick. Few use the crescent kick to attack the opponent unless they have no other choice. This kick is most often used for defensive purposes. You can apply the kick effectively in free fighting to deflect the attacking opponent's kick or hand move when, for some reason, you cannot use your arms for blocking. Sometimes, you may initiate your attacking moves by first deflecting the defending opponent's front-guarding arm with the kick and then following through with other attacks.

Deflecting the Guarding Arm. This move is performed by first deflecting the defending opponent's front-guarding arm with your rear foot and attacking with a combination move. This type of move can score against the opponent who defends mainly with arm blocks in a side-facing posture.

While the opponent is waiting for your initial move in order to counterattack with a straight reverse punch in an opposite-side-facing position, you may precede the move with a crescent kick, deflecting his front-guarding arm. The deflection should be a surprise move, putting him temporarily into an awkward position for his counter punch. Your whole body must advance with the kick, and your combination attack of the knife-hand strike must be executed instantly in order to score.

Deflecting the Kicking Leg. Assuming that your opponent attacks with a front-thrust kick and you are, for some reason, not prepared to safely arm block the kick, you can deflect the kicking leg with a crescent kick. To deflect the kick with your front foot, first raise it and swing it to your right while simultaneously bending the knee slightly to pull the kicking foot gradually toward the front part of your body. Then, cock the leg back to your body and deliver a side kick with the same foot.

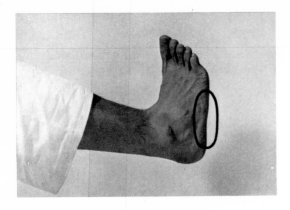

● Outer-Edge-Crescent Kick

The outer-edge-crescent kick is made with the outer edge of the kicking foot in a circular motion for both offense and defense. This kick is delivered in the opposite direction from that of the regular crescent kick. This type of kick can usually be applied, following the deflection of the opponent's front-guarding arm, to kick his face or middle target area.

In order to make an outer-edge-crescent kick in forward stance with the rear foot, cock the kicking foot in front of the left leg with the edge of the foot facing forward and the body in a half-front-facing posture. Then, deliver the outer-edge-crescent kick to your right in a circular motion by first raising the knee and swinging the hips. Your body rotates slightly to your right into a half-front-facing posture while kicking with your right foot. Stop the kicking foot at the body line with the knee slightly bent and cock it back directly to the body line.

When to Use the Kick. The outer-edge-crescent kick is applied in free fighting in the same way as the crescent kick. It can be used to deflect the opponent's kicking leg or his guarding arms in exactly the same manner. It differs from the crescent kick in that it is delivered from the reverse direction, and the deflecting surface is the outer edge. This kick is seldom expected to have a strong impact at the point of contact. However, this kick can score because it comes unexpectedly from an oblique direction.

When the defending opponent tightly guards his front-facing area in response to your initial attacking motion (your adjustment for distance or your deflection of his guarding arm to deliver a rising heel kick) you can initiate your attack with the outer-edge-crescent kick. Cock the kicking leg in front of the right leg while rotating your body slightly to the left. Then, raise the knee and deliver the kick to the opponent's face in a circular motion and cock it directly back to your body.

Index